PUBLIC RELATIONS
AND
COMMUNITY

PUBLIC RELATIONS AND COMMUNITY

A Reconstructed Theory

Dean Kruckeberg
Kenneth Starck

PRAEGER

New York
Westport, Connecticut
London

HM
263
.K69
1986

Library of Congress Cataloging-in-Publication Data

Kruckeberg, Dean.
    Public relations and community : a reconstructed theory / Dean
Kruckeberg and Kenneth Starck.
    p.   cm.
    Bibliography: p.
    Includes index.
    ISBN 0-275-92911-6 (alk. paper)
    1. Public relations—United States.   2. Community.   3. Public
relations—Missouri—Sugar Creek—Case studies.   4. Public
relations—United States—Petroleum industry—Case studies.
I. Starck, Kenneth.   II. Title.
HM263.K69   1988
659.2—dc19
                                87-30536

Library of Congress Catalog Card Number: 87-30536
ISBN: 0-275-92911-6

First published in 1988

Praeger Publishers, One Madison Avenue, New York, NY 10010
A division of Greenwood Press, Inc.

Printed in the United States of America

The paper used in this book complies with the Permanent
Paper Standard issued by the National Information Standards
Organization (Z39.48—1984).

10   9   8   7   6   5   4   3   2   1

For Maggie

Contents

Preface

This manuscript has had a magnificent journey. The trip has taken the better part of a decade. In one form or another, it has traversed the Peoples' Republic of China, crossing Asia into Europe via the Trans-Mongolian International Express Train from Beijing across Siberia to Moscow. It has stopped off in Finland and India. The route has included Oregon and Maryville, Missouri, and Minnesota and Illinois and, of course, Iowa. One is tempted to ask whether the authors always work so slowly or simply like to travel. The answers: no and yes.

The germ of the book was a graduate research project. But the project has taken a life all its own. We wish to acknowledge the contributions of many colleagues and friends to the life of the work. Sometimes such contributions have taken place inadvertently and been absorbed in the totality of the thought processes. In other instances, the contribution has been explicit and, we hope, duly acknowledged. For any merits this work may have we are deeply indebted to many persons. Any shortcomings or deficiencies of the work can be blamed only on the authors. Fortunately, when two are involved, they can blame each other.

Herewith, acknowledgments by both authors: Lary Belman, Jim Carey, Dennis Corrigan, John Erickson, Les Moeller, and William Zima, colleagues who have provided intellectual stimulation and moral support; Maynard Cuppy and Nancy Parizek, who make complex production problems seem simple; Paula Floyd, Elaine Finch, and Yu Xu, who stepped in at the last minute to help out; Alison Bricken and Karen O'Brien, the kind of editors whom authors appreciate; and anonymous evaluators of early manuscript drafts who saw sparks of promise and offered valuable criticism.

And by Dean Kruckeberg: Hanno Hardt and James Price, for early guidance; Jerry W. Cooper of Standard Oil Company (Indiana), now named Amoco Corporation; Stan Salva of Sugar Creek; Doug Newsom, Bill Brody, Norm Nager, and Jon Hall, valued academic colleagues; the waitresses in truckstops between Cedar Falls and Iowa City who served coffee and got public relations theory in return; and especially my mother and children, Stephanie and Jeremy.

And by Kenneth Starck: Don Smith, Linda Smith, and family members, who suffer the most.

Introduction

The proposition argued in this book is that a fundamental reason why public relations practice exists today is the loss of community resulting from new means of communication and transportation. Both the history and the definitions of public relations, as they are usually presented today, are inadequate. Histories have not taken into account the larger social forces operating in the environment, especially communication technology and transportation. Those who have charted the evolution of public relations tend to settle on simple, unidimensional explanations.

Rhetoric aside, public relations is commonly practiced today as a vocation utilizing persuasive communication to obtain a vested goal on behalf of a represented client. That goal is usually defined vaguely as goodwill, though it is often linked to marketing objectives. We disagree with the premise on which such operational definitions are based as well as public relations goals as they are usually operationalized. Our theory is that public relations is better defined and practiced as the active attempt to restore and maintain a sense of community. Only with this goal as a primary objective can public relations become a full partner in the information and communication milieu that forms the lifeblood of U.S. society and, to a growing extent, the world.

We make our arguments within the framework of a particular specialization of public relations, namely, community relations. Community relations was chosen, *not* because it relates directly to "community" as we define it. Instead, we enter the discussion along the path of community relations because community relations is: (1) generally recognized as one of the most important areas of public relations practice; and (2) among the most typical areas in the application of public relations skills.

Our theoretical arguments derive from the writings of the Chicago School of Social Thought. As will be shown, the Chicago School provides insights into public relations practice from a perspective that has the possibility of ameliorating theoretical and practical flaws in the conceptualization of contemporary public relations practice.

The test of a theory comes in its application. We are not aware of any organization that has designed a community relations program with the specific and express purpose of fostering a sense of community, at least to the extent that we call for. However, we have examined the theory in a case study covering 75 years of the Standard Oil Company (Indiana) refinery at Sugar Creek, Missouri.

For many readers, what follows may seem overly theoretical and abstract. That is by necessity. There are many practical examples of the points we bring up. The problem is that practical examples more often than not represent the antithesis of the position we argue.

In Part I we maintain that public relations practitioners do not understand their most important role in society. That role is to serve not only their clients but society at large. We take a critical look at the literature dealing with public relations. What emerges is an inconclusive portrait of the public relations practitioner as a professional. We explore the origins of public relations and examine ways in which it has been defined. What is lacking, we conclude, is a conceptualization of public relations that adequately takes into account social and historical elements. The Chicago School of Social Thought offers reconceptualization possibilities, largely on the basis of sense of community.

Part II deals with those factors, notably transportation and communication, that have transformed our communities as well as the way we think about them. We critically examine the notion of the Great Community espoused by the social theoreticians of the Chicago School. Despite limitations, the grandiose notion of the Great Community has possibilities that link the communication efforts of public relations practitioners with the related notion of community.

In Part III we try to reconcile our reconceptualized notions of public relations and community. We do this within the framework of the Sugar Creek case study. It is not a study in the usual behavioral mode, that is, development of hypothetical propositions followed by collection of predefined data for empirical validation or rejection of preconceived notions. Rather, we have burrowed from within, seeking evidence across the spectrum of individuals and activities associated with the community and the organization. As much as possible, the evidence creates the story. Results reflect both positively and negatively on the company's community and public relations programs and, in our estimation, point toward new directions for public relations. The need to develop community figures prominently in our conclusions.

A note about the research site of Sugar Creek: it was not an ideal site for the investigation. That is because the ideal site does not exist. For ideals—like many things—have a way of changing. "Progress," noted Oscar Wilde, "is the realization of utopias."

For the present, our conclusion, perhaps radical or naive or both, is that those who take public relations seriously, professionals as well as scholars, should not view public relations as a means of "us"—communication specialists—simply doing something to "them"—targeted publics. Instead, those responsible for public relations should approach communication as a complex, multiflow process having the potential to help create a sense of community.

PART I
THE QUANDARY OF
PUBLIC RELATIONS

It is now recognized that, unless there be in every transaction a spirit of cooperation, a spirit of "live and let live," a well-considered intention to render a service, business cannot endure and prosper.

1928 Standard Oil advertisement

1
The Historical Foundation in Question

The attitude of U.S. business toward the public has changed greatly since the robber baron era of the late nineteenth and early twentieth centuries. No doubt business's goals remain much the same; the primary goal is still maximum profit. However, for many reasons—social, economic, political, and technological, among others—the many publics in our democratic society are—and must be—reckoned with not only by business but by all types of organizations.

The person primarily responsible for this reckoning is the public relations practitioner, a twentieth century phenomenon. Parts of the job resemble that of a journalist-communicator, an applied social and behavioral scientist, a social worker, and a press-agent. Concern about "publics" and public opinion has spawned the public relations practitioner; and, to a great extent, the public relations practitioner has spawned concern about public opinion.

Although public relations as a field has become popular, almost faddish, the position and role of the practitioners in society may not be so secure as they would like to believe. Their history is vague at best and tawdry at worst. The practitioners' role today is often ill-defined, and theirs is often the first position to disappear in times of organizational retrenchment. Practitioners' attempts at professionalism have not been so successful as they would have people think. Even the manifold attempts at defining public relations have accentuated the distance that must yet be traveled before practitioners fully understand their function in society.

Despite a few voices to the contrary, public relations practitioners generally and readily accept persuasion and advocacy as their major function. As such, they point to their predecessors in the art and science of persuasion, who have left today's practitioners with a legacy of which they are not always so proud.

Conventional public relations literature takes great pains to argue that public relations is as old as civilization. The history of the human race records the vital role of persuasion within a framework of communication among individuals in society. Human societies are hardly conceivable without tools of persuasion to enable groups to make decisions and resolve conflicts. The theory and practice of communication reflect an abiding interest in the means to persuade.[1]

Persuasion and a rudimentary concern about public opinion have been evident throughout the history of civilization. Because most public relations authors strongly link public relations with persuasion, they can point with some validity to such widespread activities throughout world history as antecedents to contemporary public relations.

From the dawn of civilization, efforts to persuade and advocate were of most interest among governments and their rulers. However, public relations' more legitimate, but nevertheless more shameful, predecessor—press-agentry—really began about 1830 with the advent of the penny press. Promoters developed a talent for "making news," that is, securing media coverage, sometimes at the expense of truth and dignity.[2]

Cutlip, Center, and Broom observe:

> To state that public relations has evolved from press-agentry, though a gross oversimplification, contains a kernel of truth. Systematic efforts to attract or divert public attention are as old as efforts to persuade and propagandize. Much of what we define as public relations was labeled press-agentry when it was being

used to promote land settlement in our unsettled West, or to build up political heroes.[3]

Public relations historians searching out a past can point to these beginnings, as no doubt could political scientists, sales personnel, marketing/advertising professionals, and a host of other professions, disciplines, and callings where the ability to persuade is the key to success.

However, public relations authors argue, if politics and press-agentry were important to the evolution of public relations, it was after the Civil War that significant social change occurred, which brought about the need for public relations as it is commonly practiced today. The frontier disappeared. The nation's efforts were toward industrial and commercial expansion. Science, invention, and technology revamped the nation's economy. Oil, iron, steel, railroads, electricity, and the internal combustion engine—among many other transportation and communication breakthroughs—revolutionized the age.[4] Laissez-faire economic attitudes exemplified the era, and the robber barons of industry took control.[5] However, there was strong reaction from many within society.

Heibert observes:

> For a time during the second half of the nineteenth century, industrial leaders turned to monopoly as a solution to their economic problems. By the turn of the century, however, a reversal was taking place, largely as the result of a new kind of communication that appealed to mass man: "yellow journalism" with its practice of "muckraking." This gave to such anti-industrial groups as the agrarians and the grangers, populists, labor unions, and progressives a new power over public opinion that allowed them to counterbalance the might of the industrial captains, for a while even threatening the continued existence of their power by bringing into question the basic idea of free enterprise.[6]

Goldman notes:

> The communications revolution meant a new, wide-open boulevard to the public mind. . . . Large segments of the population

were now irritably questioning the whole role of large-scale industry and commerce in American society. They believed that big businessmen made too much money, exercised a baleful influence in politics, and operated usually as a force against the general welfare.[7]

Thus, what really prompted the birth of contemporary public relations, according to many public relations authors, was the reaction against the muckrakers with their new power to communicate with the masses. Public relations—as the concept is used today—is seen primarily as a twentieth century phenomenon. Business people began asking themselves whether traditional policies of secrecy were really the wisest course. If publicity was being used so effectively to attack business, why could it not be used equally well to explain and defend business.?[8]

By 1924 the *Chicago Tribune* was saying that public relations was becoming a profession, art, and science. The newspaper urged that in "seeking the co-operation of the public he [the business person] should first of all give the fullest co-operation to his public relations department. This means utter frankness, access to all facts, and speed."[9]

Individual authors divide up the history of twentieth century public relations practice in different ways, but basically they try to show a progression and growing sophistication in the practice of public relations. Certainly by the 1960s, if not sooner, public relations practitioners were seeking out a broader knowledge of the social sciences.[10] Also, more frequently used were methods to measure public opinion. Mathematics, statistics, and computer science had become common tools for supposedly increasingly sophisticated performance by public relations practitioners.[11]

Cutlip, Center, and Broom write:

> The history of public relations is meaningful only when it is related to these power conflicts and recurring crises of change. For example, it is not mere coincidence that in the past, business interests have taken public relations most seriously when their positions of power were challenged or threatened by the forces

of labor, the farmer, the small shopkeeper, or a maturing generation.[12]

Thus, we have a widely accepted version of the evolution of public relations. Its history, as it is usually presented and accepted by scholars and practitioners, best defines public relations as a vocation utilizing persuasive communication to obtain vested goals on behalf of a represented client. For some, public relations would impact directly on the function of marketing, though there is disagreement on this point. Seitel, for example, writes, "Whereas *marketing* and *sales* have as their primary objective to sell an organization's products, public relations attempts to 'sell' the organization itself."[13] Dunn points to the growing liaison between marketing and public relations and notes, "Although the term *marketing* is most commonly associated with the selling of goods and services, it has been applied increasingly to the non-profit field—often under the term *social marketing*."[14]

The confusion over marketing and public relations is understandable given the overall emphasis on persuasion. Nolte and Wilcox describe marketing and public relations as parallel functions and make this distinction: "Marketing sells goods and services. Public relations 'sells' policies and actions. In each case there must be a determination of what the public wants."[15]

For our purposes, such distinctions are not relevant. Whether one speaks of advertising or marketing or public relations, the concern here is with persuasion and, in a larger context, communication. For, regardless of the semantic quagmire, the point is that public relations in many respects exists today in much the same form as it existed in antiquity.

It would be grossly unfair to paint a picture of public relations today as consisting of hucksterism and propaganda as it was often practiced in the past. Yet, to many people, the distinction would be blurred.

While the manifold and essentially similar histories of public relations tend to be accurate, as far as they are developed, and while they do provide some insight into the practice of contemporary public relations, they also illustrate very well some inherent problems. They consider public relations practice to be evolutionary and progressive, continually increasing in its sophistication and professionalism. Overall, the literature, including dissertations and theses, indicates a paucity of interest in the history of the field, though public relations histories of specific organizations and practitioners abound. The *1987 Bibliography for Public Relations Professionals* does not contain a "history" category and lists only four books under "Biography/Memoirs."[16]

Several authors offer thoughtful insights into the history of public relations. Aronoff and Baskin, for example, suggest public relations evolved through three stages: from (1) manipulation to (2) information to (3) mutual influence and understanding. Significantly, they note that while the stages generally have been sequential all three have coexisted from the beginning.[17]

Grunig and Hunt have identified four evolutionary models in the history of public relations. The first, growing out of "public relations–like activities," evolved from 1850 to 1900 and is referred to as the "press agent/publicity" model. This was followed by the "public-information" model, which continued as the major model from about 1900 to the 1920s. Then followed what they term the "two-way asymmetric" model. Finally, during the 1960s and 1970s, a "two-way symmetric" model emerged. They also note the wide disparity in contemporary practice and assert that many practitioners still operate from old models, estimating that today only 15 percent of organizations follow the two-way symmetric model.[18]

Arguments can be made that public relations practice—despite more sophisticated tools and better-educated professionals—has not been so evolutionary and progressive. This is evidenced in part today by the confusion about public relations, among both educators and professionals—even at the most basic levels of agreeing on a definition and the role and function of modern public relations.

More important, public relations historians do not adequately view the underlying reasons why public relations developed and the reasons why the function seems necessary today. Some critics express skepticism over the "progressive" interpretation that affects public relations histories. Olasky observes:

> First, we are all familiar with the common view that American public relations practice has improved sharply since the "press agent" era of the nineteenth century or even the "bad old days" early in this century. Second, we also have listened to numerous liberal sermonettes about how corporations have done better at serving "the public interest" as they have spent more time relating to their public (or "publics"), as they have done more "boundary spanning," as they have developed professional contributions functions and learned to dicker and deal in Washington.[19]

Too many simple assumptions have been made about public relations' supposed evolution and progression. These assumptions do not provide a sufficient theoretical base for the practice of contemporary public relations. This becomes evident in the confusion that inevitably results in trying to define public relations.

2
The Problem of a Definition of Public Relations

Symptomatic of the inadequacies of any understanding of the role and function of public relations today is the problem of its definition. What is public relations? What does it do? What is it supposed to do? Is it doing what it is supposed to do?

Indicative of the evolving nature of contemporary public relations, as well as the muddled thinking about the field, is the seemingly infinite number of definitions proffered by those actively concerned about the status and future of public relations. Almost all definitions contain the notion of a planned effort to build and hold goodwill. This ordinarily translates into a management function designed to analyze problems, counsel clients or appropriate decision-makers, and implement "effective" communication programs.[20]

One author begins by pointing to what public relations is not: "It is not merely publicity; it is not merely propaganda; it is not advertising; it is not interference with the legitimate flow of news; it is not evasiveness; it is not the manufacturing of benefits where none exist; and it is not a refuge for slick operators or amateurs."[21]

Another author notes that, because public relations practitioners work in many different ways for many different causes, vague definitions will result, such as: public relations is any situation, act, or word that influences people.[22] Public relations is seen as planned, persuasive communication designed to influence significant publics: "The key words here are 'planned,' 'persuasive,' 'communication,' and 'significant publics.' Public relations is not accidental, but is carefully planned. It is persuasive because someone wants someone else to do something or to believe something. It may communicate to particular groups of people rather than to scattered individuals."[23]

Here are other typical definitions of public relations:

> Public relations is the management function that identifies, establishes, and maintains mutually beneficial relationships between an organization and the various publics on whom its success or failure depends.[24]

> Public relations is finding out what people like about you and doing more of it; finding out what they don't like about you and doing less of it.[25]

> Public relations is the skilled communication of ideas to the various publics with the object of producing a desired result.[26]

> good performance publicly appreciated because adequately communicated...the management function designed to increase profits, or the equivalent, directly or indirectly, by earning public goodwill through the adoption and continuing communication to the public of policies and procedures acceptable or beneficial to all concerned.[27]

There are more. Another author cites three facets of public relations: (1) information given to the public; (2) persuasion directed at the public to modify attitudes and actions; and (3) efforts to integrate attitudes and actions of an institution with its publics and of publics with that institution.[28]

An early and widely-accepted definition of public relations was developed by *Public Relations News*, a weekly newsletter: "Public relations is the management function which evaluates public attitudes, identifies the policies and procedures of an individual or organization with the public interest, and plans and executes a program of action to earn public understanding and acceptance."[29]

In 1976 Dr. Rex F. Harlow sought to develop, once and for all, a really comprehensive definition. With funding provided partly by the Foundation for Public Relations Research and Education, he collected 472 definitions of public relations. He eventually derived two definitions, a "Descriptive Definition" and this "Working Definition":

> Public relations is a distinctive management function which helps establish and maintain mutual lines of communication, understanding, acceptance and cooperation between an organization and its publics; involves the management of problems or issues; helps management to keep informed on and responsive to public opinion; defines and emphasizes the responsibility of management to serve the public interest; helps management keep abreast of and effectively utilize change, serving as an early warning system to help anticipate trends; and uses research and sound and ethical communication techniques as its principal tools.[30]

This was an admirable effort at comprehensiveness. Yet Harlow's definition would hardly be the last. In August 1978 the "Statement of Mexico" was adopted. It read: "Public relations practice is the art and social science of analyzing trends, predicting their consequences, counseling organization leaders, and implementing planned programs of action which will serve both the organization's and the public interest."[31] This definition, which was approved at the World Assembly of Public Relations meeting in Mexico City, was endorsed by 34 national public relations organizations.[32]

Other authors express yet other ideas. Nolte argues rightly that, because a public relations program can no longer be based entirely on adapting the environment to the organization, it must give equal attention to adapting the organization to the environment. Using this "ecological concept," he defines public relations as "the management function which adapts an organization to its social, political, and economic environment and which adapts that environment to the organization, for the benefit of both."[33]

Robinson took a decidedly behavioristic approach in his 1966 book:

> Public relations as an applied social and behavioral science is that function which:

1. measures, evaluates, and interprets the attitudes of various relevant publics;
2. assists management in defining objectives for increasing public understanding and acceptance of the organization's products, plans, policies, and personnel;
3. equates these objectives with the interests, needs, and goals of the various relevant publics; and
4. develops, executes and evaluates a program to earn public understanding and acceptance.[34]

Aronoff and Baskin argue that public relations

is a management function that helps to define organizational objectives and philosophy and facilitate organizational change. Public relations practitioners communicate with all relevant internal and external publics in the effort to create consistency between organizational goals and societal expectations. Public relations practitioners develop, execute, and evaluate organizational programs that promote the exchange of influence and understanding among organizations' constituent parts and publics.[35]

Norris stresses simplicity and breadth in his definition. He says public relations is "having relationships with people" and coins the apt phrase "public relationships."[36]

Crable and Vibbert define public relations as "the multiphased function of communication management that is involved in researching, analyzing, affecting, and reevaluating the relationships between an organization and any aspect of its environment."[37]

Dunn says public relations is a "management function that uses two-way communication to mesh the needs and interests of an institution or person with the needs and interests of the various publics with which that institution or person must communicate."[38]

Moore and Kalupa argue that public relations is "a social philosophy of management expressed in policies and practices, which, through sensitive interpretation of events based upon two-way communication with its publics, strives to secure mutual understanding and goodwill."[39]

Brody emphasizes the business aspect. He observes: "Public relations has become less an art or science and more a business. More precisely, management of the *practice* has become as important as management of the *process*."[40]

Nager and Allen, who argue that public relations should be practiced through a management by objectives (MBO) approach, point to the ceaseless quest for an appropriate definition of public relations and point out that each new generation of attempts "has led to more emphasis on the management role."[41]

As Seitel points out, the many definitions of public relations aid in trying to understand the scope of the practice. The lack of agreement, he suggests, indicates that public relations is a continually evolving field.[42] On that point there might be extensive agreement.

After only a sampling of the many and diverse ways in which public relations is explained or defined, the principle of diminishing returns—apart from exhaustion—sets in. Nonetheless, we think it instructive to mention one more. It comes from Grunig and Hunt. Public relations, they say, is "management of communication between an organization and its publics."[43] The simplicity of the definition masks the depth and comprehensiveness of what they advocate. They argue for a "two-way symmetric" model of public relations based on negotiation, compromise, and understanding. The authors, drawing on systems theory, elaborate on the two-way symmetric model:

> Practitioners serve as mediators between organizations and their publics. Their goal is mutual understanding between organizations and their publics. These practitioners, too, may use social science theory and methods, but they usually use theories of communication rather than theories of persuasion for planning and evaluation of public relations. . . .
>
> The two-way symmetric model . . . consists more of a dialogue than a monologue. If persuasion occurs, the public should be just as likely to persuade the organization's management to change attitudes or behavior as the organization is likely to change the publics' attitudes or behavior. Ideally, both management and publics will change somewhat after a public relations effort.
>
> Frequently, however, neither will change attitudes or behav-

ior. The public relations staff brings the two groups together, and, as long as both communicate well enough to understand the position of the other, the public relations effort will have been successful.[44]

Through these many definitions run several common threads. As long ago as 1979, Nolte identified these basic themes among public relations definitions: planning, social responsibility, two-way communication, honesty, and performance.[45] Today one would add management.

While all these definitions undoubtedly have some validity in describing how public relations is practiced today, and thus perhaps contribute to an understanding of its practice, they also demonstrate the overall lack of precision in contemporary practice, to the extent that practitioners and scholars cannot even agree on the function of public relations.

More important, most definitions exemplify a concern for the client being allowed to exist and prosper within the client's environment. This, perhaps more than anything else, justifies in a highly pragmatic manner contemporary public relations practice.

The definitions presented in this book come from a much larger universe. Essentially, with the few exceptions noted, they render public relations as a vocation utilizing persuasive communication to obtain a vested goal on behalf of a represented client.

Definitions, it might be argued, have limited practical value. Yet definitions, at least those held in common, are necessary for any intelligent discourse; they help to determine the universe of that discourse. This review of definitions of public relations suggests vagueness and disagreement and confusion. Often the definitions fall victim to their own complexities in attempts to be both comprehensive and socially justifiable. If anything, such definitions best illustrate that, to understand public relations as it is commonly practiced today, it is necessary to look at what public relations practitioners do, not at what they attempt to define their job to be.

3
Conclusions about an Inconclusive Vocation

Examining what public relations practitioners do also can be problematic. Job descriptions are based on the perceived need for public relations, what Ross summarizes for a great many other authors as "an investment in the privilege to operate."[46] The Public Relations Society of America declares: "Public relations helps our complex, pluralistic society to reach decisions and function more effectively by contributing to mutual understanding among groups and institutions. It serves to bring public and public policies into harmony."[47]

Whether because of such concerns as self-survival and prosperity or because of more altruistic—but undoubtedly secondary—reasons, public relations continues in great demand in this country and, increasingly, throughout the world. One author cites an increase from about 19,000 public relations practitioners in 1950 to more than 150,000 in 1986.[48] Another source reports 384,000 persons working in 1984 as public relations managers, representatives, or specialists.[49] Estimates that more than half a million persons are engaged in public relations work are not unrealistic.

Expenditures on public relations efforts in the United States amount to $10 billion a year.[50] Most large U.S. companies have public relations departments, while many other companies retain public relations agencies. The 1985 *O'Dwyer's Directory of*

Public Relations Firms lists 1,600 public relations agencies and public relations departments of advertising agencies.[51]

In many other rapidly developing parts of the world, public relations interest is poised at a take-off stage. For example, in China, where one of the authors spent a year teaching, associations of public relations practitioners have sprung up in Shanghai and Beijing and elsewhere. In addition, universities and colleges throughout the nation are rushing to develop instructional programs and materials.

Enrollments in U.S. schools of journalism and mass communication also reflect the exploding interest in public relations. For several years now public relations and advertising have become increasingly popular career choices among students interested in the communication professions.[52] Universities and colleges have been quick to exploit the general interest in public relations as well as the relative vagueness in the practice of public relations. The range of the programs is extremely broad in focus, and the resulting curricula vary tremendously.

A decade ago Denny Griswold, editor and publisher of *Public Relations News*, predicted, "In the changing world where the actions of business, religion, education, government, and other sectors of the American system are being judged before the bar of public opinion, public relations is essential, its role, assured, and its future, bright."[53] Her words were prophetic.

The practice itself is most often reduced to a formulated process, at least among those providing textbook answers to public relations problems. Although authors will devise their own formulae, most adhere basically to a derivation of the RACE formula, introduced by John E. Marston in 1963. This is: Research, Action, Communication, and Evaluation.[54] Such formulae take a problem-solving approach—which today is advocated almost universally, in theory at least—as opposed to pure publicity-seeking by press-agents, publicists, and many information specialists. A considerable number of practitioners who pay lip service to such a problem-solving approach, however, may be nothing more than press-agents in practice.

Such formulae usually elevate the function of public relations to a management policymaking level and emphasize the need for research and evaluation, activities unknown to many early public relations practitioners. In addition, such formulae recognize the importance of both performance and communication in the development and maintenance of good public relations. Most authors and practitioners believe public relations practiced in this way, in fact, can be carried on effectively in a professional, ethical, and socially responsible way. Indeed, many feel that following such practice represents the primary criteria in the conduct of what is believed to be "real" public relations.

Such formulae translate into an almost infinite number of specified tasks. The Public Relations Society of America describes public relations activities as: (1) programming; (2) relationships with others; (3) writing and editing; (4) information; (5) production; (6) special events; (7) speaking; and (8) research and evaluation.[55]

Textbook authors report essentially the same types of tasks, but categorize them in several different ways. Practitioners also frequently divide up their tasks into concern for various publics. Cole points out that a practitioner could easily compile a list of 50–100 different publics for any given organization, depending on how specifically one wants to categorize publics.[56]

A critical analysis of the literature, however, reveals that an adequate understanding of public relations requires more than a perusal of the endless numbers of definitions espoused by public relations authors. It requires more than accepting the perceived need for its practice, a need most evident on the part of the organizations that employ public relations practitioners and perhaps far less so on the part of the publics on which the organizations are focusing.

To understand public relations likewise requires more than memorization of the sundry formulae, most of which are similar in intent and content. And providing a typology of activities proves difficult, if not meaningless. Public relations practitioners perform an endless variety of activities—which indicate that public relations as it is practiced today essentially amounts to a vocation utilizing persuasive communication to obtain vested goals on behalf of a represented client. Such a definition admittedly makes public relations no more than an ambiguous umbrella term for an endless number of tasks and for a large number of specializations and related fields.

We see that attempts to describe public relations—its definition, role, and function—evoke more questions than answers. Histories generally present public relations as the practice of persuasion among those in power—or those seeking power—and sketch the practice of public relations as a distinct organizational function, which nevertheless remains almost hopelessly broad. Myriad definitions share some degree of similarity, but most demonstrate an overall lack of precision in understanding. Meanwhile, public relations is fairly well accepted, suggesting fulfillment of a need that goes beyond the mere need to persuade. There would seem to be a more fundamental explanation for the existence of public relations—perhaps lying in broader social and societal need.

Likewise, formulae for practicing public relations are descriptive and useful, yet simplistic and inadequate. To describe public relations by citing a range of possible activities and possible publics becomes either too restrictive to apply to all organizations' practice or too broad to be meaningful.

Public relations today—despite increasingly sophisticated tools—operates from much the same perspective as it did before the term was even used. Organizations want to survive and prosper. Adverse public opinion—especially in a free and democratic society—can threaten such survival and prosperity, while positive public opinion can help assure survival and prosperity. Therefore, public relations practitioners attempt to develop and maintain positive public opinion, or at least to neutralize negative public opinion, within the context of the liberal-plural tenets of U.S. democracy. To accomplish this, they use persuasion and good works in an attempt to influence both the emotional and rational factors contributing to public opinion formation.

Most typically today practitioners rely on a combination of attempts to assure a good environment for the represented client. Such attempts include a simplistic concern for altruistic good citizenship, a concern with the dynamics of public opinion formation and change within a highly behavioristic conceptual framework (and which promises to increase with the greater numbers of practitioners educated in the behavioral sciences), and a simple, usually nontheoretically-grounded, emphasis on the techniques of involvement with the organization's various publics.

It is time for us to ask a basic question: Does the history of public relations, as it is commonly presented, adequately or even accurately describe why public relations exists today?

Our argument is that a fundamental reason public relations practice exists today is because of a loss of community resulting from new means of communication and transportation. Public relations practitioners for years have addressed and attempted to remedy symptoms and not deal with basic problems of society, and, more specifically, their clients' relationships to the various elements of society.

Another question: What is an appropriate definition of public relations, its role and function?

The preceding discussion has noted the vagaries and the inadequacies of most present definitions and has concluded that public relations as it is commonly practiced today is little more than a vocation utilizing persuasive communication to obtain vested goals on behalf of a represented client.

Our conclusion is that the present approach to public relations activities are not wrong but represent superficial and insufficient consideration of underlying propositions. Or, to put it another way, we think the articulation of public relations depends on an explanation growing out of historical and social forces. And, thus, we posit—which for practical purposes should be regarded as a working definition of public relations—that public relations is the active attempt to restore and maintain a sense of community.

4
A Framework of Community Relations

We have asked two questions: Does the history of public relations as it is commonly presented adequately or even accurately describe why public relations exists today? And, what is an appropriate definition of public relations, its role and function?

We will address these questions within the framework of a particular specialization of public relations, namely, community relations. This approach makes sense because community relations, among all the various activities and specializations of public relations, is among the most important and among the most typical in the application of public relations skills. Therefore, community relations is our focus. Our conclusions, however, will have much broader relevance. It is our contention that the conclusions can be applied to the generalized practice of public relations itself.

In public relations parlance, a community is most often thought of as the city or area where the organization is physically located. Employees, customers, stockholders, suppliers, and many other key "publics" of the organization may be located within the same "geographic public." Therefore, practitioners will sometimes describe the community as all those who do not have a direct financial interest in the organization, although these members of the geographic public might have a considerable secondary financial interest.[57]

Practitioners argue, and many organizations apparently believe, that people today expect an increasing sense of social responsibility from industry and commerce. Some note that the purpose of the community relations function is to keep on good terms with the community as a whole and with key individuals in the community as well as to be a good corporate citizen.[58]

Community relations is an organization's planned, active, and continuing participation with and within a community to maintain and enhance its environment to the benefit of both the institution and the community.[59]

Community relations includes a great many activities, including the primary function of recognizing and carrying out the company's social responsibilities in the community.[60] The aim of a community relations program is to establish a line of communication through words and deeds that are carefully planned to make the company a partner in the community.[61]

A program of community relations, in short, must establish and nurture the best possible climate in which the organization can operate.[62]

For our purposes, the word "community" has greater depth than it does in these examples from the traditional public relations literature.

Despite the amount of rhetoric that public relations authors devote to community relations—including explanations of the function and the need for community relations as well as what an organization can do for its community—public relations practitioners involved in community relations must address more specifically why their organizations should even be concerned about community relations. The arguments, at the base level, once again become a pragmatic discussion of survival.

Koch says that a community relations program offers everything to gain and everything to lose.[63] He says that it is simply good business. The success/failure of a company's community relations program, which is essentially nonmarketing in its orientation, can affect its profits—which are related to the community relations program in several ways, including the amount of property taxes and other taxes, zoning restrictions, employee loyalty, and the quality of new employees. Peak uses a useful analogy, despite its offensively sexist nature:

> Business marries the community it settles with. It takes on inherent responsibilities with this association. The need for community relations today might be seen as a wife (community) taking a close look at the marriage vows and discovering her husband (business) owes her more than simple financial support (taxes). Let him ignore or refuse his marital responsibilities and the husband has the neighbors (public opinion) and the courts (local government) to contend with.[64]

Any organization within the community has a great many ways to serve the community, if such is its strategy in its community relations practice. These different activities, to varying degrees, can encourage goodwill on the part of the community toward the organization. Intuitively, it would seem that such organizations would realize their organizational goals through such activities. The resultant goodwill would allow a positive and peaceful climate in which the organization could survive and prosper. Likewise, such programs of community relations would provide benefits to the members of the community public.

However, an examination of the community relations literature does little to refine the definition we advocate for public relations in general. Community relations seems to be practiced for the same reasons as is public relations for other publics. That is, adverse public opinion at the community level can threaten survival and prosperity. On the other hand, positive public opinion can help assure survival and prosperity.

The specific literature of community relations is grossly deficient and inappropriate for the same reasons that other public relations literature is deficient and inappropriate. Moreover, if the term "public relations" is so broad and ill-defined as to be meaningless, the derivative term "community relations" poses the same difficulties. In fact, the concept of "community" as used in community relations literature is an overwhelming misnomer. As it is typically referred to in the term "community relations," it is not really a community. It might be more accurately called a "geographic public." Public relations practitioners are not practicing community relations as we advocate that it should be practiced. Rather, they are simply utilizing persuasive communication to obtain a vested goal for their client, and this goal is directed toward a geographic public.

At face value, this contention may appear to be nothing more than a confusing exercise in semantics. However, the distinction is worth noting because much of the nation's social and organizational dislocation occurred at about the same time that modern public relations evolved. This would seem to be more than coincidence. The social upheaval resulted from loss of a sense of community, a loss due, in large part, to new technology—which changed human relationships as it changed modes of communication and transportation. Modern public relations—which justifies its role and function in part because of the deficiencies of modern society—does not address itself specifically to the problem of restoration and maintenance of community. Rather, public relations practitioners seek out—increasingly with the aid of the social scientist's tools—seemingly sophisticated methods to create a favorable public opinion climate for the represented organization, supposedly for the benefit of that organization's publics. The effort does not directly address underlying problems.

An alternative approach to community relations is one that directly stimulates and activates attempts to restore and maintain a sense of community, which has been lost in contemporary society. Such an approach requires practitioners to view community (and public) relations and its role and function from another perspective, one that is more abstract but with a deeper philosophical base.

5

A Theoretical Framework: The Chicago School of Social Thought

Public relations practitioners point to their function as being mutually beneficial to their clients and to their clients' various publics, primarily because of their supposed efforts at two-way communication. But many professionals pay only lip service to such practices and only adopt feedback devices to develop more sophisticated persuasion techniques. Likewise, in the arena of community relations, practitioners extol the virtues of a well-run community relations program designed to bring mutual benefits to the represented organization and to the geographic populace. However, as noted, the approach is narrow and excludes vital elements within its focus.

Public relations experts do recognize that contemporary society is complex and that such complexity fosters various types of maladjustments. In addition, they do argue generally that public relations practice can perhaps overcome some of these maladjustments and at the same time fulfill the primary goal of assuring a good public opinion environment for the represented client. But the experts do not satisfactorily address how public relations can help resolve what is actually the more important problem: loss of community. Public relations practitioners have been so preoccupied with superficial, obvious, and pragmatic goals that they have not considered other avenues that promise even greater benefits to their organizations and society as a whole. It is, after all, the larger environment in which public relations must function.

Are other approaches feasible? Why should an organization take on responsibilities using a considerable amount of its own resources to help resolve societal problems that appear—on the surface—to offer little or at least limited direct benefit to the organization itself? Also, to even entertain the idea of another approach such as is being advocated here, where must a practitioner begin? If restoration and maintenance of community are the goals of community (and public) relations, how should the problem be approached?

One place to begin is the Chicago School of Social Thought. These scholars, with whom public relations practitioners and scholars are relatively unfamiliar, were engrossed with the question of loss of community. Their insights seem as valid today as when they first considered this and other social issues at the end of the nineteenth and the beginning of the twentieth centuries. A few public relations texts, in fact, do make brief but highly limited use of some ideas popularized by the Chicago School. The use is restricted to dealing with only a few concepts, such as "the public" as conceived by John Dewey.

The sociologists in the Chicago School of Social Thought consisted mostly of a group of professors at the University of Chicago. An exception was Charles Horton Cooley, a University of Michigan professor whose intellectual interests and philosophies were similar to those at the University of Chicago. Central figures in the Chicago School included John Dewey, George Herbert Mead, W. I. Thomas, Robert E. Park, Thorstein Veblen, Ernest Watson Burgess, and Louis Wirth.[65]

The group became collectively known as the "Chicago School" because of their common interests and because all but Cooley spent much of their academic careers at the University of Chicago. In addition, many used the City of Chicago as a laboratory for their study of society.[66] The period of the Chicago School, at least of its greatest productivity and influence, was from 1892 through about 1939.[67]

Although the Chicago School had no direct interest in the practice of public relations, much of what it had to say seems directly relevant to the practice of public relations, perhaps not in how it is routinely practiced today nor in how it is presented theoretically, but in how it could be practiced with an overall goal of restoration and maintenance of community. Within a comparatively narrow span of time, there occurred not only the loss of community and the beginnings of modern public relations, but also the beginnings of the Chicago School of Social Thought and a concern about loss of community.

The Chicago Scholars rued the loss of community as exemplified through modern means of communication and transportation, through industrialization and urbanization. They sought to regain their ideal of what had been lost. They attempted to do this through the means by which they perceived community as having been lost to begin with. What they sought and how they attempted to seek it are worthy of consideration by anyone seriously interested in public relations.

Ironically, the Chicago School sought to restore community primarily through the original culprit—communication. The widespread use of mass media, which was impersonal in nature, combined with easy and cheap long-distance communication among individuals, altered people's relations to one another. One solution, the scholars felt, was utilization of the new technology to open up new and replace old channels of communication. Communication, after all, is the quintessential component of public relations. The Chicago School, we believe, can provide the theoretical framework from which contemporary public relations practitioners can achieve what we believe should be their primary goal, namely, restoring and maintaining community.

The next part of this book will analyze the loss of community in contemporary U.S. society. The sense of community that existed a century ago is no longer common. This is due, in large part, to the advent of modern means of communication and transportation. The America of the mid–1800s was an America of small-town life, a lifestyle idealized by scholars of the Chicago School as well as by others. Eventually, however, the city became the place where most Americans would live. And the overall impact of the city was the atomization of individuals.

Public relations scholars have tended to avoid specific concern for this and for related social problems. But the Chicago

School did not. The Chicago School dealt actively with such issues. Although the school's "Great Community" did not come about, much of what it advocated serves as a useful guide for public relations practitioners in restoring and maintaining a sense of community.

Notes for Part I

1. Doug Newsom and Alan Scott, *This is PR: The Realities of Public Relations*, 3rd ed. (Belmont, Calif.: Wadsworth Publishing Co., 1985), pp. 28–29.

2. Ibid., pp. 27–28.

3. Scott M. Cutlip, Allen H. Center, and Glen M. Broom, *Effective Public Relations*, 6th ed. (Englewood Cliffs, N.J.: Prentice-Hall, Inc., 1985), p. 27.

4. Edward L. Bernays, *Public Relations* (Norman: University of Oklahoma Press, 1977), p. 50.

5. Ibid., p. 51.

6. Ray Eldon Hiebert, *Courtier to the Crowd: The Story of Ivy Lee and the Development of Public Relations* (Ames: Iowa State University Press, 1966), p. x.

7. Eric F. Goldman, "Public Relations and the Progressive Surge: 1898–1917," *Public Relations Review* 4 (Fall 1978): 55.

8. Ibid., p. 58.

9. Cited in Bernays, *Public Relations*, pp. 93–94.

10. Newsom and Scott, *This Is PR: The Realities of Public Relations*, pp. 50–51.

11. Ibid., p. 53.

12. Cutlip, Center, and Broom, *Effective Public Relations*, pp. 23–24.

13. Fraser P. Seitel, *The Practice of Public Relations*, 3rd ed. (Columbus, Ohio: Merrill Publishing Co., 1987), p. 8.

14. S. Watson Dunn, *Public Relations: A Contemporary Approach* (Homewood, Ill.: Irwin, 1986), p. 12.

15. Lawrence W. Nolte and Dennis L. Wilcox, *Effective Publicity: How to Reach the Public* (New York: John Wiley & Sons, 1984), p. 5.

16. *1987 Bibliography for Public Relations Professionals* (New York: Public Relations Society of America, 1987), p. 5.

17. Craig E. Aronoff and Otis W. Baskin, *Public Relations: The Profession and the Practice* (St. Paul, Minn.: West Publishing Co., 1983), p. 15.

18. James E. Grunig and Todd Hunt, *Managing Public Relations* (New York: Holt, Rinehart and Winston, 1984), pp. 25–26.

19. Marvin N. Olasky, "Public Relations vs. Private Enterprise: An Enlightening History Which Raises Some Basic Questions," *Public Relations Quarterly* 30 (Winter 1985): 6.

20. Robert T. Reilly, *Public Relations in Action* (Englewood Cliffs, N.J.: Prentice-Hall, Inc., 1981), p. 10.

21. Ibid., p. 1.

22. John E. Marston, *Modern Public Relations* (New York: McGraw-Hill Book Co., 1979), p. 5.

23. Ibid., pp. 3–4.

24. Cutlip, Center, and Broom, *Effective Public Relations*, p. 4.

25. Cited as an inadequate definition, but which indicates the need for research and action, in John E. Marston, *Modern Public Relations*, p. 6.

26. Cited as an inadequate definition, which stresses communication but not deeds, in Ibid., p. 6.

27. Among examples or definitions cited in Reilly, *Public Relations in Action*, p. 4.

28. Bernays, *Public Relations*, p. 3.

29. Definition from *Public Relations News*, 127 East 80th St., New York, N.Y. 10021, edited and published by Denny Griswold. This definition was formulated more than 40 years ago by the editors of *Public Relations News* and is used here with permission from Denny Griswold.

30. Rex F. Harlow, "Building a Public Relations Definition," *Public Relations Review* 2 (Winter 1976): 34–37.

31. Raymond Simon, *Public Relations: Concepts & Practices*, 3rd ed. (New York: Macmillan Publishing Co., 1986), p. 6.

32. Dennis L. Wilcox, Phillip H. Ault, and Warren K. Agee, *Public Relations: Strategies and Tactics* (New York: Harper & Row, 1986), p. 6.

33. Lawrence W. Nolte, *Fundamentals of Public Relations: Profes-*

sional Guidelines, Concepts & Integrations (New York: Pergamon Press, 1979), p. 10.

34. Edward J. Robinson, *Communication and Public Relations* (Columbus, Ohio: Charles E. Merrill Publishing Co., 1966), pp. 51–52.

35. Aronoff and Baskin, *Public Relations: The Profession and the Practice*, p. 9.

36. James S. Norris, *Public Relations* (Englewood Cliffs, N.J.: Prentice-Hall, Inc., 1984), pp. 1–3.

37. Richard E. Crable and Steven L. Vibbert, *Public Relations: As Communication Management* (Edina, Minn.: Bellweather Press, 1986), p. 5.

38. Dunn, *Public Relations: A Contemporary Approach*, p. 5.

39. H. Frazier Moore and Frank B. Kalupa, *Public Relations: Principles, Cases, and Problems*, 9th ed. (Homewood, Ill.: Richard D. Irwin, Inc., 1985), p. 5.

40. E. W. Brody, *The Business of Public Relations* (New York: Praeger, 1987), p. 1.

41. Norman R. Nager and T. Harrell Allen, *Public Relations: Management by Objectives* (New York: Longman, 1984), p. 6.

42. Seitel, *The Practice of Public Relations*, p. 15.

43. Grunig and Hunt, *Managing Public Relations*, p. 6.

44. Ibid., pp. 22–23.

45. Nolte, *Fundamentals of Public Relations: Professional Guidelines, Concepts & Integrations*, p. 9.

46. Robert D. Ross, *The Management of Public Relations: Analysis and Planning External Relations* (Melbourne, Fla.: Robert E. Krieger, 1984), pp. 10–11.

47. Formally adopted by the Public Relations Society of America (PRSA) Assembly, November 6, 1982.

48. Joseph R. Dominick, *The Dynamics of Mass Communication*, 2nd ed. (New York: Random House, 1987), p. 348.

49. Study by Professor Robert L. Kendall, University of Florida, cited in Wilco, Ault, and Agee, *Public Relations: Strategies and Tactics*, p. 4.

50. Joseph F. Awad, *The Power of Public Relations* (New York: Praeger, 1985), p. 3.

51. Jack O'Dwyer, *O'Dwyer's Directory of Public Relations Firms: 1985* (New York: J. R. O'Dwyer Co., Inc., 1985), p. 5.

52. Paul V. Peterson, "Enrollment up 7 Percent in '86, Outstripping University Growth," *Journalism Educator* 42 (Spring 1987): 4–5.

53. Interview with Denny Griswold reported in "After 30 Years," *Public Relations Quarterly* 22 (Spring 1977): 11.

54. James A. Files, "RACE: A Public Relations Process Model for Orderly Planning and Efficient Implementation," *Public Relations Journal* 38 (July 1982): 22–25. This offers an excellent summary.

55. Cited in Ronald P. Lovell, *Inside Public Relations* (Boston: Allyn and Bacon, Inc., 1982), p. 6.

56. Robert S. Cole, *The Practical Handbook of Public Relations* (Englewood Cliffs, N.J.: Prentice-Hall, Inc., 1981), pp. 4–5.

57. Nolte, *Fundamentals of Public Relations: Professional Guidelines, Concepts & Integrations*, p. 227.

58. Ross, *The Management of Public Relations: Analysis and Planning External Relations*, p. 169.

59. Wilbur J. Peak, "Community Relations," in *Lesly's Public Relations Handbook*, 3rd ed., Philip Lesly, ed. (Englewood Cliffs, N.J.: Prentice-Hall, Inc., 1983), p. 70.

60. Ross, *The Management of Public Relations: Analysis and Planning External Relations*, pp. 171–172.

61. Arnold Koch, "On the Street Where You Live," *Going Public* (March 1981): 52.

62. Ibid.

63. Ibid.

64. Peak, "Community Relations," p. 70.

65. Sheldon Lary Belman, "The Idea of Communication in the Social Thought of the Chicago School" (Ph.D. dissertation, University of Illinois at Urbana-Champaign, 1975), pp. 1, 96.

66. Ibid., pp. 1–2.

67. Ibid., p. 3.

PART II
A SENSE OF COMMUNITY

The kids have a good sense of family and home, and thereby family and home have a priority over professional or occupational success. . . . These values are picked up or "caught" rather than taught.

Sugar Creek Resident

6
Sense of Community No Longer Common

The sense of community that existed a century ago is no longer common. This is in large part because of modern means of communication and transportation. Human beings develop social systems, and communication plays an essential part in the creative processes of this development. Technology and culture are also critical elements. In the interplay of social life and a changing environment, communication systems do not exist frozen in time or outside social space. Change is constant; rate of change is variable.

Today's mass communication systems were influenced by forces and events culminating during the time from about 1890 to World War I. It was about the same time that modern public relations began. Unfortunately, technological developments inevitably run ahead of our ability to understand their social impact. Thus, the way we think about modern communication systems and the role of such systems in contemporary life tends to be rooted in the past.

The University of Chicago was founded in 1892. The scholars within the Chicago School of Social Thought were perhaps the first to consider collectively and systematically the role of communication in society. The school's findings and philosophies provided remarkable insights into the U.S. society of that time—and beyond.

But this particular time period is significant for another reason. It was a time of tremendous change in the United States, both in the way people lived and in the way they communicated. During this era, innovations in communication technology and transportation altered the social fabric of the nation. New technology left its imprint, as did accelerated use of older technologies: the railroad; the telegraph and ocean cable; the post office with its rural free delivery; and then the automobile and truck, together with improved roadways. Aviation was a dramatic new means of travel. It would not be long before radio would be ready for mass use.

By the 1890s, still other means of communication and transportation had emerged and were being commonly used or were soon to have an impact on society. These included canals, the steam-driven cylinder press, photography, the manufacture of inexpensive paper from pulpwood, photoengraving, the phonograph, and the motion picture projector.[1] And the typewriter, invented earlier, began to find its own special niche in a society increasingly driven by communication.[2]

These new means of communication and transportation brought change to life in the cities as well as in the remote countryside. What had been predominantly "island communities" changed drastically—vanished, in fact—because of the changes in transportation and communication. Americans were being transformed into a mass society interconnected by a maze of communication and transportation that yielded both blessings and curses. The new communication and transportation nationalized the country and at the same time resegmented it. The old structures of community life gave way to something that exists in similar but even heightened form to this day. People no longer identified with their immediate "neighborhood" but rather were melting into the larger pot of Americana, and maybe even into the global village.

The island communities' local economies also changed. Farmers could use the railroads to send their produce to parts unknown. Manufacturers could produce not only enough to meet the needs of their own communities but as much as regional, national, and international markets could absorb. Dependency replaced the self-sufficiency of the island communities. Specialization of production was possible to a degree not previously known. Through mass markets, a wide range of consumer goods became available—which encouraged a certain physical and, relatedly, a cultural similarity. Boorstin remarks, "In the twentieth century Americans would be the best-clothed and perhaps the most homogeneously dressed industrial nation."[3]

But change produced its own headaches. People gradually became aware of the control they had surrendered. Railroad rates were arbitrarily set by someone they did not know. Local jobbers could not compete in a new system that allowed wholesale houses to supply a basic line of groceries and dry goods throughout an area. Few merchants could offer more flexible conditions of credit than they themselves received. The local banker was drawn into an enlarged world of finance, allowing neither local merchant nor banker to borrow on an informal basis any longer.[4]

And with this interdependence came a homogenization of America and Americans. The nationalization of communication and transportation systems was largely responsible for mass culture.

Nationalization of communication meant large numbers of people would be exposed to the same information in the same magazines and newspapers, which—to an increasing extent— were served by the same writers and wire services and news syndicates. They would receive this information at about the same time. They would read the same advertisements, which attempted to influence them in a like manner. They would hear the same political messages. The media would present them with similar lifestyles and values. Power and influence seeped in from outside the community. National media cut across structural divisions within local societies, drawing audiences from all races, creeds, occupations, and social classes.

But if nationalization was homogenizing Americans in certain ways, it was also doing something else. Mass society with its mass culture was creating new divisions, especially along occupational lines. People of the same vocational and professional interests did not have to be close physically to communicate and to identify with one another. Bonded by similar interests, they became nationally reconstituted by and through

new means of communication and swift and easy transportation. Media that could hurdle time and space to reach everyone
could also be used to communicate selectively with people who
were scattered geographically.

Even as internally homogeneous and stable as communities
of the 1870s were, there were distinctions that provided individuals with their own identities. In a democracy where every
person could manage just about every task, no one achieved
distinction from the exclusivity of his or her livelihood. Moreover, those who shared similar vocational talents and interests
but were dispersed geographically did not know one another
and therefore could not act together.[5]

The specialized needs of a culminating urban-industrial economic and social system gave people an identity through their
professions and occupations. Such identification gave them the
deference of their neighbors, while the increasingly formal entry requirements protected their occupations' prestige.[6] A new
middle class of specialists and professionals emerged as a result
of the new means of communication and transportation. They
developed their own professional communities, which were
spread out in geographic space, but were homogeneous communities nevertheless. Such groups replaced the deteriorating
loyalties of the geographic island communities.

However, the recreated and realigned communication systems that culminated during the time from about 1890 to World
War I did more than nationalize and resegmentize U.S. society.
These systems also inverted the relationship of public life and
private life. The middle class at the end of the nineteenth century was withdrawing from the streets, from the public meeting
places. When they went to public places, they used these places
in private ways. Print, because of growth in literacy and
through national distribution, tended to be used as a private
means of communication. Increasingly, mass communication
came to be regarded as a private act of communication, without
the group discourse common in earlier times.

Individuals tended to become anonymous to others around
them. This anonymity was later heightened by the privately-
owned automobile and the department store, self-service store,
"super" drugstore, and supermarket.[7] The rise of the radio

made the relationship between seller and buyer less direct because it was difficult to tell who was listening.[8] The insurance company replaced, or rather displaced, the old community. Rather than living in the "real" communities of the 1870s, people were being grouped into statistical categories and considered in terms of demographic characteristics.

Americans, beginning from the time of about 1890 to World War I, became isolated and privatized. Modern transportation and communication forms allowed them to learn and travel by themselves, to go to public places where they would not be known, and to commune privately with those escorting them. Americans today can stay at home and read the newspaper, watch television programs, including a surfeit of cable channels, or use a home television set to watch inexpensive video-recorded movies. The radio is omnipresent. Americans can travel alone in their automobiles to an impersonal supermarket. If an individual's garage burns down, he or she can telephone an insurance claim service to have an adjuster estimate damages. In modern mass society, the American has become a homogeneous, segmented, and deeply private individual.

Professional communicators, including public relations practitioners, must take into account these social changes and try to understand their ramifications. Public relations practitioners must have an expanded sense of history and an appreciation of contemporary needs to be able to conceptualize their task and to understand the unique role they can play.

The need for modern public relations evolved, at least in part, as a result of these social factors and not merely as an expedient and pragmatic response to the muckraking exposures of the evils of rampant industrialization and big business. People themselves have changed. Their society and social systems have changed. A significant factor in their change was in the means of communication and transportation. Public relations historians, by and large, have not adequately traced these roots. Nor have they taken into account the importance of such changes to the practice of public relations.

7

The Shift from Rural to Urban Life

Most of the concerns of public relations practitioners today simply did not exist before the loss of community. For it was this loss of community that provided impetus for the development of modern public relations. The obvious goals of public relations practitioners—persuasion and advocacy—were, at an earlier time, concerns primarily of politicians, governments, and promoters, whose organizational goals were different from those espoused by most contemporary public relations practitioners. Then, public relations consisted mainly of press-agentry—with the specific and blatant objective of acquiring political power or material gain, such as through land sales. Today public relations practitioners concern themselves primarily with relationships between and among groups and with solving problems usually related to communication.

Public relations, it could be argued, came about to fill a social vacuum created by the disappearance of community. On this point, our data are only suggestive. A concurrent emphasis on material consumerism also spurred the development of public relations. But just as important, it seems to us, was the need for people to be put back into touch with their changing environment. Public relations helped to fulfill that need.

The America of the mid–1800s was an America of small-town life, a lifestyle now idealized by many. This was the norm before the loss of the island communities and their dependence on the satellite farms and ranches and other small industries that provided their economic support.

Sparse population densities throughout most of the nation unquestionably contributed to the search for community, if for no other reason than the fact that most people did not want to face the alternative of loneliness. Search for community in this country was both manifest and realized from the time of the first immigrants. Communities existed before governments.

The primary group relationships extending over an area the size of a small town appeared to function best in isolated situations. There the division of labor was relatively simple, and the cultural and racial composition of the population was homogeneous. McKenzie noted:

> In rural areas neighbors are likely to be intimately acquainted; common feelings and sentiments are shared regarding questions of local group welfare. Here relationships are quite similar to those in larger families in that much is held in common and shared, one member with another.[9]

Although a homogeneous culture and common heritage of folkways and mores did not necessarily permeate communities when they first began taking shape, cohesiveness invariably set in as the communities developed and matured. Living in such early communities offered a style of life vastly different from what we experience today. There was an intimate relationship between: (1) the local, kinship, and religious groups within which individuals consciously lived; and (2) the major economic, charitable, and protective functions necessary for human survival. The individual had a sense of membership in society. Family, church, and community drew and held the allegiances of the individual because of their apparent and overt relationship with the economic and political order.[10] There was control over the immediate environment and comparative security of economic position.[11] Personal and neighborhood affairs were the staple of conversation.[12] The small, isolated rural towns made public decisions in an atmosphere of local consensus.

Groups of these towns fell into satellite patterns around the few larger urban centers from which they sought markets, supplies, credit, and news. But these communities managed to confine the sense of living largely within themselves. Relatively few farm families lived so far from town that they did not gravitate to some degree into its circle. The towns—usually homogeneous and Protestant—enjoyed an inner stability. There was neither an aristocracy of name nor of occupation.[13]

Modern means of communication and transportation destroyed all this. Small towns lost their appeal as vital communities and became backwaters. The focus of power shifted to the metropolitan areas. Small towns found that there were few important decisions left for them to make. The big issues were being resolved in Washington, New York City, Chicago, and—to a lesser extent—the state capitals.[14] Many small communities stagnated, with much of their natural population growth fleeing. The younger generation and more enterprising individuals noted the lack of opportunities in their hometowns. When such towns declined in population because of a weakening economic and social base, disorganization and social unrest often followed. Competition became keener within the community. And the weaker elements were forced either into a lower economic level or withdrew from active participation in the affairs of the community.[15]

The city was where the future of most Americans lay. Yet cities were always looked on as inherently evil. In advocating an agrarian democracy, Thomas Jefferson had warned about an impending decline in medical, moral, and political conditions—which he felt was spawned by the cities.

But cities were inevitable. They grew out of marketplaces, political capitals, forts, places of worship, and transportation rest stops. Cities also fostered economic specialization. Their growth led from the simple to the complex, from the general to the specialized. The U.S. metropolis crossed the threshold from the earlier gemeinschaft community based on fellowship to the modern gesellschaft society based on formal organization.[16]

To the city came concentrated industrial, commercial, financial, and administrative facilities and activities, as well as transportation and communication lines and cultural and recreational activities.[17] With the growth of great cities, with the vast division of labor that derived from the earlier machine age, and with the movement and change that came about with the multiplication of the means of transportation and communication, the old forms of social control represented by family, neighborhood, and local community were undermined, and their influence was greatly diminished.[18]

The major difference between the city and the island communities on which the nation was built came to be reflected in the loss of community. The urban lifestyle had several effects. It weakened bonds of kinship, family, and neighborhood. It undermined the traditional basis for social solidarity.[19] To the city came new varieties of contact and communication, largely the result of and influenced by the decreasing division of labor and the growing diversity of cultures and races.[20] Fortuitous and casual relationships replaced more intimate and permanent associations. The individual's status under such circumstances was determined more by fashion and front.[21] Social distances were maintained in spite of geographical proximity; relations among neighbors were more aptly described as symbiotic rather than social.[22] People in cities lived together not because they were alike, but because they were useful to one another.[23]

The overall impact of the city was the atomization of individuals, that is, the pulling away of people from a cohesive social center. Kornhauser identifies three "democratic criticisms" of the drift toward a mass society: (1) growing atomization (or loss of community); (2) widespread readiness to embrace new ideologies (the quest for community); and (3) totalitarianism (total domination by a pseudocommunity).[24]

To urban people who took their vocations to be their identities, involvement in the neighborhood was of little importance. Nevertheless, the urban dweller often tended to become a joiner of voluntary organizations to compensate for the community that had been lost. According to Wirth, it was largely through the activities of voluntary organizations that the urbanite could express and develop a personality, acquire status, and be able to carry on the round of activities that constitutes a life's career.[25]

Other scholars have explored problems associated with social change, and some have addressed the varied implications of the social problems resulting from the changes described here.

DeFleur and Ball-Rokeach, for example—drawing on the work of French sociologist Durkheim—note that, as society becomes more complex and people become more preoccupied with their own individual pursuits and development, they lose the ability to identify with others and to feel part of a community. They become inward-oriented and linked to others primarily through contractual ties.[26]

Klapp observes that people can be busily involved in a mass society yet still show a chronically low level of genuine concern for others. The breakup of small groups contributes to this eroding personal concern. Such small groups as extended family, clan, tribe, village, and parish have not been replaced by the associations of modern times—such as labor union, political party, church, or social set. A vacuum sets in. He concludes:

> It is not surprising that lack of concern goes with a[n] . . . element in the context of modern identity problems: *shallowness of feeling*, inability to feel sentiments strongly or to sense that one is living fully. . . . Emotion is privatized. Everyone is trying to be cool; it is becoming embarrassing to express feelings openly, "wave the flag," be homesick, "wear one's heart on one's sleeve." Perhaps a reason is lack of emotional support.[27]

Nisbet argues that there is a decided weakening of faith in the inherent stability of the individual and in the psychological and moral benefits of social impersonality. Impersonality, moral neutrality, individualism, and mechanism have become terms to describe the pathological conditions of society.[28] Lawler suggests that, with society becoming more and more dominated by large, complex organizations, it is important to recognize the unique worth of each human being.[29] Nisbet adds that interpersonal relationships are as abundant in our age as in any other, but it is apparent that for more and more people such relationships are morally empty and psychologically baffling:

> It is not simply that old relationships have waned in psychological influence; it is that new forms of primary relationships show, with rare exceptions, little evidence of offering even as much psychological and moral meaning for the individual as do the old ones. For more and more individuals the primary social relationships have lost much of their historic function of mediation between man and the larger ends of our civilization.[30]

Nisbet points out that this theme of the individual uprooted without status and struggling for revelations of meaning and seeking fellowship in some kind of moral community is recurrent. In an earlier age the individual gained release from the pressure of certainty and triumphed over tribal or communal laws of conformity. The common notion today is of an impersonal, even hostile, society—a society in which all actions and motives seem to have equal value and to be perversely detached from human direction.[31]

Swanson notes that there are many who fear the destruction of human values if three factors—urbanism, industrialization, and bureaucratization—are not better controlled and modulated in the interests of the human community. Public and private leaders are expected to play a major role in regulating such exigencies. However, he observes, this American pragmatic response to the problems of urban growth is both insufficient and ineffective.[32] Francois asserts that rapid social, technological, and economic changes have characterized our society for decades. Increased mobility led to the nuclear family. Mass society, mass production, mass transportation, and mass media all contribute to the individual's feeling of loneliness and alienation in a world becoming increasingly impersonal.[33]

DeFleur and Ball-Rokeach see mass society characterized by individuals presumed to be psychologically isolated from each other. Impersonality in interactions with others allows one to be relatively free from the demands of binding informal social obligations.[34]

Klapp refers to the strong but confusing impact of the times on the identity of modern youth. The white-collar worker's career is seen as unheroic, boring, and restricted—a dreary shuttling between the rat race of business and the tame existence of suburbia. The pileup of irrelevant information in a technological-scientific society has become an overload in education—boring and irrelevant, killing students' interest. Youth finds the same irrelevance in the community, unless they restrict their attention to some narrow band of stimuli that suggests an intense and meaningful life. Thus, young people are caught in a dilemma between an actually rather drab career outlook and the unrealistic, inappropriate, sometimes demoralizing career goals offered by celebrities as models via mass communication. When such an explosion of wishes created by mass communication is not met by realistic career opportunities, frustration follows.[35]

Factors identified by Klapp as contributing to such identity frustrations of the middle class in mass society are destruction of home environment, loss of contact with tradition, lack of ceremonies recognizing the individual, lack of social concern, weakening sentiments, and confusion of aspiration. He warns: "No amount of pile up of wealth and welfare services is going to solve these problems unless focused on improving meaningful relationships of people to each other and to their home environments, thus reducing psychological and spiritual frustrations."[36]

8
The Chicago School and the Search for Community

The social problems cited in the preceding chapter do not receive much attention in the literature of public relations. They should. In fact, they should receive primary attention because of the social centrality of the public relations enterprise. Scholars associated with what came to be known as the Chicago School recognized such problems in their time and attempted to deal actively with them.

Members of the Chicago School believed that history was fundamentally progressive and that the study of communication was the primary means toward understanding social phenomena. One writer has described the Chicago School scholars as "strongly historical in orientation; optimistic in mood, though rueful in context; and democratic and humanitarian in spirit."[37]

The evolution of the large city fascinated, yet frightened, these scholars. They feared the breakdown of the small, close-knit group due to urbanization and industrialization. Family, neighborhood, and small-town solidarity were being replaced by the ties of the marketplace. Physical unity was being newly created by the division of labor and modern communication and transportation, and a corresponding moral unity had not yet emerged.[38] Chicago School scholars took as their task the study of modernization and its ramifications on social life. They saw the biggest challenge of the twentieth century as the conversion, in Dewey's words, of the Great Society into the Great Community. Despite the social dislocation brought about by a society turned mass, they believed it was possible to sustain the distinctive elements of a community existence and achieve one large community.

Critical to our discussion is the notion of community. Chicago School scholars dwelt at length on the concept of "community" and the related term "society." Burgess noted that the terms "society," "community," and "social group" were being used with a certain difference of emphasis, but with little difference in meaning.[39] He maintained that "society" is the more abstract and inclusive term and is made up of social groups, each possessing its own specific type of organization, but having at the same time all the general characteristics of society in the abstract.

"Community," on the other hand, is the term applied to society and social groups when they are considered from the point of view of the geographical distribution of the individuals and institutions of which they are composed.[40]

> It follows that every community is a society, but not every society is a community. An individual may belong to many social groups but he will not ordinarily belong to more than one community, except in so far as a smaller community of which he is a member is included in a larger of which he is also a member. However, an individual is not, at least from a sociological point of view, a member of a community because he lives in it but rather because, and to the extent that, he participates in the common life of the community.[41]

The internal organization of any given social group, according to Burgess, will be determined by its external relation to other groups in society. Equally influential are the relations of individuals within the group to one another. Examples could include a boys' gang, a girls' clique, a college class, or a neighborhood just as much as a labor union, a business enterprise, a political party, or a nation.

Yet people do not become a community merely because they live in physical proximity. A community is achieved when people are aware of and interested in common ends and regulate their activity in view of those ends. Communication plays a vital role as people try to regulate their own activities and to participate in efforts to reach common ends.[42] Individuals, he said, are chiefly interested in entering into the activities of others and taking part in conjoint and cooperative doings. Otherwise, Dewey argued, no such thing as a community would be possible.[43]

Mead conceived of community and the democratic ideal as an entity comprised of functionally interdependent and integrated individuals, which he said was possible in modern life if caste systems segmenting society could be eliminated. Mead believed that the ideal of human community rested on the attainment of functional differentiation and social participation.[44] He observed:

> Within our communities the process of civilization is the discovery of these common ends which are the bases of social organizations. In social organization they come to mean not opposition but diverse occupations and activities. Difference of function takes the place of hostility of interest. The hard task is the realization of the common value in the experience of conflicting groups and individuals. It is the only substitute. In civilized communities while individuals and classes continue to contend, as they do, with each other, it is with the consciousness of common interests that are the bases both for their contentions and their solutions.[45]

Park noted that the simplest description of a community is a collection of people occupying a more or less clearly defined area.[46] He warned, however, that a community is more than that—not just a collection of people, but also a collection of institutions. Institutions, not people, he said, are final and decisive in distinguishing the community from other social constellations. Likewise, there is always a larger community. Every community is part of some larger and more inclusive one, with the ultimate community being the world.

As compared to society, Park said, community more accurately describes the social organism as Spencer conceived it. Community, in the broadest sense, has a spatial and geographical connotation. Every community has a location, and the individuals in the community have a place of residence within the territory that the community occupies. Individuals also have a place in the local economy.[47] Park noted that the community, if not always identical with society, is at least the habitat in which societies grow up. It provides the economic organization and the necessary conditions in which societies are rooted, on which they can be established.[48] Thus, Park considered the community as a population that is territorially organized and more or less completely rooted in the soil it occupies, with its individual units living in a relationship of mutual interdependence that is symbiotic rather than societal.[49]

Park made other distinctions about the community. For example, he pointed to its ecological organization, that is, the distribution of population and institutions.[50] Too, the community may be conceived in terms of the effects of communal life in a given area on the formation or maintenance of a local culture, that is, those sentiments, forms of conduct, attachments, and ceremonies characteristic of a locality that have either originated in the area or become identified with it. This Park called the "cultural community."[51] He held that it was in the community where formal organizations such as the church, school, and courts came into existence and had their separate functions defined.[52]

Park observed that people who compose a community and participate in common enterprises will have a body of common memories sufficient to enable them to understand one another.[53] Too, the community is where individuals maintain not only their existence as individuals, but also their lives as persons.

> The community, including the family, with its wider interests, its larger purposes, and its more deliberate aims, surrounds us, incloses us, and compels us to conform; not by mere pressure from without, not by the fear of censure merely, but by the sense of our interest in, and responsibility to, certain interests not our own.[54]

The human community has its inception in the traits of human nature and human needs. Humans cannot live alone. Besides such basic needs as shelter and protection, they need the company of other humans.[55] Individuals find themselves at home in their community only gradually as they succeed in accommodating themselves to the larger group, incorporating into the specific purposes and ambitions of their own lives the larger purposes of the society in which they live.[56] Mead observed that, until people can respond to themselves as the community responds to them, they do not genuinely belong to the community.[57]

Park noted a distinction between family and community. Familial society seems to exist to perpetuate the race, thus being instinctive, while communal society has arisen from the need for people to survive as individuals. Under such conditions, people have come together not from some impulse comparable to a sex instinct, but for "the more pragmatic and intelligible reason that they are useful to one another."[58]

Mead observed that the selfhood of a community depends on organization, so that common good becomes the end goals of individuals in the community.[59] Each individual in the community, according to Park, finds a suitable milieu, that is, an environment adapted to individual needs and one to which the individual can adapt.[60] Dewey said that associated—that is, joint—activity is a condition of the creation of a community.[61] However, association is physical or organic, while communal life is moral. "Moral" to Dewey meant being sustained emotionally, intellectually, and consciously.

The organization of the community depends on individuals taking the attitude of other individuals, that is, in Mead's terms, the "generalized other."[62] So far as a person takes the attitude of one individual in the group, the person has to take it in its relationship to the action of the other members of the group. If an individual is to adjust personally, he or she has to take the attitudes of all involved in the process. According to Mead, "The organization, then, of social responses makes it possible for the individual to call out in himself not simply a single response of the other but the response, so to speak, of the community as a whole. That is what gives to an individual what we term 'mind'."[63]

Thus, several elements in the Chicago School's discussion of community are useful to our consideration of public—and, relatedly, community—relations:

1. An individual ordinarily belongs primarily to one community.

2. The individual participates in the common life of the community, is aware of and interested in common ends, and regulates activity in view of those ends. For this, communication is required.

3. Functional differentiation occurs to some extent because people have diverse occupations and activities.

4. People in a community occupy a definable geographic area.

5. Institutions spring up and become prerequisites to community formation.

6. A community develops particular cultural characteristics.

These elements constitute our "sense of community" and dictate the way we employ the concept here.

According to such criteria, it is doubtful that many people in contemporary U.S. society could claim full-fledged membership in any community. Participation in the common life of the community, though subject to varying interpretation, would probably stand as the main obstruction for most people. This would be especially true in larger population areas where the majority of Americans today live. For, as Wirth observed, an increase in the number of inhabitants of a community beyond a few hundred limits the possibility of each member of the community knowing all the others personally.[64]

Despite the difficulty of arriving at lucid definitions of complex ideas, we believe that the concept of community is important. Instead of community per se, perhaps what we should refer to is what the concept of community connotes. For, whether or not public relations practitioners are aware of it, the idea of community figures prominently in the communication—hence, public relations—process.

9
Attempts to Regain Community

Chicago School scholars addressed the issue of loss of community and the attempt to regain it in a variety of ways. To a nation today swathed in MTV (Music Television) and propelled by desktop computers and schedules calibrated by the minute, some of the ideas of the Chicago School may seem old-fashioned or nostalgic. But their approach to communication remains seminal and speaks directly to contemporary society. Their concern about the restoration and maintenance of community was expressed consistently within a community-oriented framework of communication.

Dewey noted, "Democracy must begin at home, and its home is the neighborly community."[65] His response to the problem of the loss of community consisted mainly of striving to restore and develop it by having young people engage in activities central to the lives of their families and friends.[66] He believed that only through oral communication could the demands of time and democracy be met.[67] Cooley shared with Dewey an interest in the public schools in helping to create a sense of community. He also emphasized a special need to build up in the country a type of culture distinctly rural in character, yet not inferior to urban culture in its ability to enlarge life.[68] Around the school might be grouped the rural church, which would also be consolidated and socialized and made a center of fellowship and cooperation. Also important would be the public library, the art gallery, and a hall for political and social gatherings. As Cooley said, in a community enjoying such institutions with a spirit and traditions of its own, life ought to be at least as livable as in town.

Mead believed that the solution to the crisis of modern life lay in restoring the social order and ideals of traditional society. Park argued that the local community organizations must encourage a "new parochialism," seeking "to initiate a movement that will run counter to the current romanticism with its eye always on the horizon, one which will recognize limits and work within them. Our problem is to encourage men to seek the deity in their own villages and to see the social problem in their own neighborhoods."[69] Park sought to organize a community's leisure time around such activities as politics, religion, and community welfare, as well as the more obvious leisure activities of golf, bridge, and other forms of recreation.[70] Local interests and associations breed local sentiment, Park said; and under a system that makes residence the basis for participation in government, the neighborhood becomes the basis of political control.[71] The newspaper—and here we would broaden this to encompass other news media, including electronic—must continue to serve as the diary of the home community. "Marriages and divorce, crime and politics, must continue to make up the main body of our news. Local news is the very stuff that democracy is made of."[72]

The Chicago School regarded education as an important part of community, not only in and of itself, but also because of its benefits in helping to create a sense of community. Dewey's idea of the school as an "embryonic community" puts a premium on personal contact and exchange within a setting of cooperative work and inquiry. Besides being a little community for the young, the school would be a social center for the neighborhood. The school would unify the local community.[73]

The Chicago School viewed the arts, especially literature, as having particular importance in creating community:

> Art breaks through barriers that divide human beings, which are impermeable in ordinary association. This force of art, com-

mon to all the arts, is most fully manifested in literature. Its
medium is already formed by communication, something that
can hardly be asserted of any other art. There may be arguments
ingeniously elaborated and plausibly couched about the moral
and the humane function of other arts. There can be none about
the art of letters.[74]

Striving toward community would also occur in the playground. The playground should be something more than a place
for working off steam and keeping children out of mischief.
Rather it should be where children form permanent associations. Under conditions of urban life, where the home tends to
become little more than a sleeping place, the play group as-
sumes increasing importance.[75]

In a great city, children are the real neighbors; their habitat is
the local community; and when they are allowed to prowl and
explore they learn to know the neighborhood as no older person
who was not himself born and reared in the neighborhood is
ever likely to know it.[76]

Dewey saw communication as an opportunity to enhance
society. It is the means for establishing cooperation, domination, and order. He saw communication as both personally ful-
filling—or, in his word, consummatory—as well as practical—
or, again in his word, instrumental.[77] Communication is instrumental as it liberates us from the otherwise overwhelming
pressure of events and enables us to live in a world of things
that have meaning. It attains fruition as a sharing in the ob-
jects and arts precious to a community—a sharing whereby
meanings are enhanced, deepened, and solidified in the sense
of communion.[78]

Discourse itself is both instrumental and consummatory. Communication is an exchange which procures something wanted;
it involves a claim, appeal, order, direction or request, which
realizes want at less cost than personal labor exacts, since it
procures the cooperative assistance of others. Communication
is also an immediate enhancement of life, enjoyed for its own
sake.[79]

Cooley said that the secret of a stable society is simply giving all forms of energy a chance to express themselves within the system. Needed in any system are freedom and stability, which result from rational human beings behaving rationally. Thus, freedom and stability form an indivisible trinity with social intelligence.

This was considered important by others in the Chicago School. Quandt writes:

> Dewey's later writing on public opinion revealed his continuing concern with the importance of verbal communication in creating community. "Signs and symbols, language, are the means of communication by which a fraternally shared experience is ushered in and sustained," he wrote in the 1920's. But "vision is a spectator; hearing is a participator. Publication is partial and the public which results partially informed and formed until the meanings it purveys pass from mouth to mouth." Without the vitality of a close, direct interaction, he reasoned, the formal transmission of information could not carry the burden of creating mutual sympathy.[80]

Park held that the newspaper, or news media, is the great medium of communication within the city, and it is on the basis of the information it supplies that public opinion rests. The first function of news media is that formerly performed by the village gossip.[81] Mead noted the vast importance of journalistic media, since they report situations through which one can enter into the attitude and experience of other persons.[82] Cooley observed that the essential function of the news media is to serve as a bulletin of important news and as a place for the interchange of ideas through the dissemination of interviews, letters, speeches, and editorial comment. In this way, he said, a news medium is indispensable to the organization of the public mind. The bulk of its matter, however, is best described as organized gossip, which people formerly carried on at crossroad stores or over the back fence.

> There is a better and a worse side to this enlargement of gossip. On the former we may reckon the fact that it promotes a widespread sociability and sense of community. . . . It also tends pow-

erfully, through the fear of publicity, to enforce a popular, somewhat vulgar, but sound and human standard of morality. On the other hand it fosters superficiality and commonplace in every sphere of thought and feeling, and is, of course, the antithesis of literature and of all high or fine spiritual achievement. It stands for diffusion as opposed to distinction.[83]

Dewey pointed out, however, that conversation has a vital aspect lacking in the fixed and frozen words of written speech.[84] Systematic and continuous inquiry into all the conditions that affect association and their dissemination in print is a precondition of the creation of a public. But, Dewey warned, it and its results are but tools. Their final actuality is accomplished in face-to-face relationships by means of a direct give-and-take. Logic, he said, in its fulfillment recurs to dialogue. Ideas that are not communicated, shared, and reborn in expression are soliloquy; and soliloquy is broken and imperfect thought.

The Chicago School was instructive in its recognition—as well as in offering a possible resolution—of a societal predicament that remains unresolved today. At one level, one might argue that the Chicago School failed in its attempts to deal with a changing society. But its lack of success, we believe, was not because the school's observations and conclusions were wrong. Rather, the Chicago School did not succeed in its attempts because it sought to project a small-town sense of community onto mass society directly, rather than more judiciously trying to reverse the societal trends that it so astutely identified as responsible for the loss of community.

Quandt reminds us that the Chicago School, in this analysis of the uses of communication, tried to harmonize two different kinds of communication that, for later generations, do not coexist and complement one another so easily.[85] According to the Chicago School, face-to-face communication and intimate community, despite urbanization and functional specialization, would survive intact. Meanwhile, through the new means of communication, the values of intimacy and immediacy would permeate the whole structure of organized society. Quandt observes that the school's frequent reference to society as a large family was an expression of the romantic desire to personalize the entire social order. It was able to bring together the family and society aspects of community because of its belief that social evolution was moving in the direction of greater physical and spiritual unity, a movement that would require no loss of personal forms of community as it forged the Great Community.

Carey says that this belief in communication as the cohesive force in society was part of the progressive creed. Communication technology was to be the key that would improve the quality of life and turn the country into "a continental village, a pulsating Greek democracy of discourse on a 3,000-mile scale."[86] Carey draws heavily from the Chicago School's view of communication when he observes that the widespread social interest in communication today derives from a derangement in our models of communication and community. This derangement comes from an obsessive commitment—highly evident in the public relations literature, we would add—to a transmission view of communication and the derivative representation of communication in complementary models of power and anxiety.

When we think about society, says Carey, we are almost always coerced by our traditions into seeing it as a network of power, administration, decision, and control—that is, as a political order. Alternatively, Carey says, we have seen society essentially as relations of property, production, and trade—that is, as an economic order. However, social life is more. It also includes the sharing of aesthetic experience, religious ideas, personal values and sentiments, and intellectual notions—a "ritual" order.[87]

The transmission view of communication connotes doing something communicatively—persuading? advocating?—*to* someone else. The competing model, which indeed probably predates the other, stresses the "communal" or "communitarian" aspect of communication. Sometimes called "ritual," this model connotes doing something communicatively *with* someone. The theoretical implications of the two different approaches are enormous. Just as great are the implications in the realm of the practical.

Public relations early adopted—and has continued to apply—the transmission model of communication, that is, principles rooted in persuasion and advocacy rather than principles based on social involvement and participation.

10
The Chicago School's Application to Community Relations

It may be tempting to dismiss the theory of the Chicago School as unrealistic or to cite the likelihood of a Great Community as an overly-optimistic prediction. Nevertheless, the validity of much of what the school espoused is very much evident. Its literature offers a useful and instructive entry into mass communication theory, including the field of contemporary public relations. Much of what the Chicago School had to say is directly relevant to the practice of public relations, perhaps not as it is routinely practiced today nor as it is presented theoretically in most of the traditional literature, but as it could be practiced with an overall goal of restoration and maintenance of community.

The Chicago School's theoretical framework is directly applicable to community relations as well as to public relations in general. The community as a special "public" of public relations is, indeed, geographically based. Public relations practitioners can take an active part in helping community members become aware of and interested in common ends. This requires communication, in which the public relations practitioner presumably has practical expertise. Practitioners can help various publics and the organizations they represent become conscious of common interests that are the bases for both their contentions and their solutions. With conscientious thought and an appropriate theoretical base, practitioners can help individuals in the community maintain their existence as individuals and promote their worth as persons.

Certainly, practitioners—with some forethought—can help individuals in the community overcome alienation. Practitioners can help individuals accommodate themselves to the larger group in the community. They can help members of the community to know one another. They can help develop person-to-person relationships. They can help bring about a sharing of personal experiences among members of the community.

Could community relations practitioners actually help their organizations assume the role that Dewey had reserved for the public schools, that is, in helping create a sense of community? Could the great irony of the Chicago School—the prescription of more technology as a solution for the effects of technological society—become reality today with the increasing application of new capabilities in low-power television, video, and home computers?

Park's concern with leisure time in the community certainly is not well applied by most organizations, with the exception of sponsorship of softball teams and a few similar activities. Park reinforced the importance of the local news media and of local news. Public relations practitioners can take advantage of such avenues of communication, and not just for purposes of puffery. Indeed, Dewey's notion of consummatory communication represents an interesting and not necessarily idealized challenge for the public relations practitioner. Most of public relations' communication is, in fact, instrumental. Consummatory communication—for example, something pertaining to the arts—offers an immediate enhancement of life and can be enjoyed for its own sake. And there are ways the public relations practitioner can help individuals find security and protection through association with others. Why cannot the public relations practitioner help members of the community fulfill their social roles?

Dewey claimed that education is the paramount moral duty of the community. Public relations practitioners can lead their organizations in the performance of this duty. They can lead their organizations in many aspects of education beyond the more usual self-vested education in capitalism and free enterprise, which is too often preoccupied with reaffirming the status quo within an industrialized society. Dewey's concern about interest in community welfare and social order and progress can be addressed by the public relations practitioner and at a socially loftier plane than is presently done. Organizations, capitalizing on their potential as social centers, could complement the educational system through enlightened leadership by public relations practitioners. Likewise, in the area of art, public relations practitioners, through their communications expertise, could bring art and an appreciation of art to the community.

The Chicago School's belief that the playground could be an important factor in the development of community raises possibilities for public relations practitioners and their organizations. Many a facility and many a parking lot could be applied to recreational activities for youth and adults alike, especially during evenings and weekends when such facilities receive little or no use.

Why cannot the public relations practitioner help foster personal friendships? Likewise, in our mobile society, are there ways that public relations practitioners can help individuals in the community to root themselves and grow with it—gaining in depth, significance, and flavor, and absorbing the local tradition and spirit? Is it really necessary, as Cooley implies, that we must make America itself a homogeneous neighborhood, and absorb that?

Too, in the arena of news, it would behoove public relations practitioners—in their overriding concern with simply obtaining coverage—to violate, on occasion, the hallowed principle of offering up only organizationally favorable news (and thus possibly inducing a false harmony between the organization and the community). At times, should not practitioners and their organizations make the news disruptive? Certainly public relations practitioners generate a censored form of "village gossip," that is, generally positive reports about the organizations they represent. But do practitioners adequately consider other areas of information to communicate? Cooley observed that the essential function of the newspaper is to serve as a bulletin of important news and as a medium for the interchange of ideas. This does not just have to be publicity about the organization through employee publications or other media within the community.

Should not practitioners concern themselves in their communication efforts not just with ideas, but also with sentiments, attitudes, and emotions, as Park indicated, partly through the medium of conventional symbols and partly through gesture and expressive behavior, that is, behavior that can be interpreted intuitively?

Those in the Chicago School—especially Cooley, Park, and Mead—took issue with the behaviorists. Today behaviorism has become of increasing interest to many public relations practitioners. Here Cooley's dichotomy of spatial and social knowledge is instructive:

> We may ... distinguish two sorts of knowledge: one, the development of sense contacts into knowledge of things, including its refinement into mensurative science. This I call spatial or material knowledge. The second is developed from contact with the minds of other men, through communication, which sets going a process of thought and sentiment similar to theirs and enables us to understand them by sharing their states of mind. This I call personal or social knowledge. ... Spatial knowledge, we know, has been extended and refined by process of measurement, calculation, and inference, and has given rise to exact science. It is not generally agreed that knowledge of this sort is verifiable and cumulative, making possible that ever growing structure of ascertained fact which is among the proudest of human achievements. It may be worth while to consider for a moment to what this peculiarly verifiable character is owing. It is owing, I take it, to the fact that this sort of knowledge consists essentially in the measurement of one material thing in terms of another, man, with his senses and his reason, serving only as a mediator between them.[88]

In the least, this should give pause to public relations practitioners, whose research is generally of the so-called spatial type. Practitioners today seldom get to know their publics in a genuinely communicative sense. Their perceptions come to be based on the spatial level, that is, information presumed to be "objectively" measured yet communicatively distant.

Also pertinent to this point is a similar distinction that Park made between "acquaintance with" and "knowledge about." Acquaintance with, according to Park, is the knowledge individuals acquire in their personal and firsthand encounters with the world around them. Individuals come to know things not merely through their senses, but through the response of the whole organism.[89] On the other hand,

> "Knowledge about" is formal knowledge; that is to say, knowledge which has achieved some degree of exactness and precision by the substitution of ideas for concrete reality and of words for things. Not only do ideas constitute the logical framework of all systematic knowledge but they enter into the very nature of the things themselves with which science—natural as distinguished from the historical science—is concerned.[90]

What today's practitioners know about their publics is usually knowledge about, which is incomplete without acquaintance with. Practitioners are plagued by the inability to know their organizations' publics in the sense of Cooley's social knowledge and Park's acquaintance with knowledge.

The Chicago School was greatly interested in public opinion. Cooley saw the process of communication, and more particularly its embodiment in public opinion, as cementing social bonds and ensuring consensus. Cooley saw public opinion as an "organic process," not just a state of agreement or disagreement about issues. Public opinion, according to Cooley, was not a "mere aggregate of separate individual judgments, but an organization, a cooperative product of communication and reciprocal influence." It does not emerge from prior agreement, but rather from reciprocal action of individual opinions on each other, that is, from the clash of ideas in the process of communication. Public opinion is the product of communicated disagreement refined through debate and intellectual confrontation. Conflicts, said Cooley, are healthy and normal, as long as they proceed from a consensus about basic matters.[91]

This is especially important for public relations practitioners who are keenly interested in public opinion but whose barometer is merely the public opinion poll. For Dewey, such debate required face-to-face communication:

> There is no limit to the literal expansion and confirmation of limited personal intellectual endowment which may proceed from the flow of social intelligence when that circulates by word of mouth from one to another in the communication of the local community. That and that only gives reality to public opinion.[92]

Here, too, if we accept Dewey's argument, public relations practitioners would seem to be missing something vital. Most practitioners today might argue that face-to-face communication in modern mass society is inefficient, if not impossible. Yet as the perceptive Tocqueville noted long ago about a then-young America, "Means must then be found to converse every day without seeing each other, and to take steps in common without having met."[93]

Perhaps a basic beginning for scholars and practitioners interested in examining public relations from another vantage point should be from the perspective of community. Restoration and maintenance of community would then become the primary goal of today's practitioner. And this must take place through communication. The Chicago School saw the relationship between community and communication as necessary to a healthy social structure.

Regarding the staple of public relations—that is, communication—public relations people in the past frequently described themselves as "news persons." Such an attitude today is anathema to those schooled in contemporary public relations theory. Park described the public relations person as an individual who makes a profession of knowing when and how to make statements to the public and of knowing how these statements will be received. In the United States, he said, such people, together with pressure groups and the press, have more or less superseded Congress in forming public opinion and, indirectly, in making laws.[94] Most public relations practitioners would be flattered by that appraisal. Compare this with Park's concept of news, whose function, he said, is to orient man and society to an actual world. In his words: "What calls for a change in attitude or action in those communications that come to us through the newspaper is news."[95]

The fact that sense of community has become less strong in modern mass society creates a need that, we believe, the public relations practitioner can help satisfy. But such a role also makes the job of the public relations practitioner more difficult. It represents a public relations role different from the one presently practiced. Restoration and maintenance of community as a goal can be accomplished through communication beyond what is usually considered within the purview of contemporary public relations thought. Public relations authors generally argue that communication itself is no more important within the formulated approach than are research, action, and evaluation. Perhaps such formulae are a weak attempt to deal with the complexity of the process or a reaction against the press-agentry of the publicist. This narrow perspective regards communication primarily as information dissemination. It is a transmission view of communication and not the more encompassing ritualistic view advocated here.

The public relations practitioner's role as a communicator and, more specifically, as a communication facilitator should be a calling of the highest order. This is a greater and more important role than merely influencing public opinion through persuasion and advocacy. Being a facilitator of communication—ritual communication in a broad sense—is a role of critical importance today; it can help build a sense of community among members of an organization and the community public. Such a role does not indicate a lesser need for education, professionalism, prestige, or anything else that public relations practitioners and scholars have worked to achieve over the years. It does require a new perspective, a different theoretical base, and an attempt to come to grips with the ills that plague contemporary society.

Notes for Part II

1. Sheldon Lary Belman, "The Idea of Communication in the Social Thought of the Chicago School" (Ph.D. dissertation, University of Illinois at Urbana-Champaign, 1975), pp. 12–13.

2. Edwin Emery and Michael Emery, *The Press and America: An Interpretative History of the Mass Media*, 5th ed. (Englewood Cliffs, N.J.: Prentice-Hall, Inc., 1984), p. 231.

3. Daniel J. Boorstin, *The Americans: The Democratic Experience* (New York: Vintage Books, 1974), p. 92.

4. Robert H. Wiebe, *The Search for Order: 1877–1920* (New York: Hill and Wang, 1967), pp. 48–49.

5. Ibid., p. 113.

6. Ibid.

7. Boorstin, *The Americans: The Democratic Experience*, pp. 107, 116–117.

8. Ibid., p. 154.

9. R. D. McKenzie, *The Neighborhood* (Chicago: University of Chicago Press, 1923), p. 348.

10. Robert A. Nisbet, *Community and Power* (London: Oxford University Press, 1967), pp. 53–54.

11. Charles Horton Cooley, *Social Organization: A Study of the Larger Mind* (New York: Charles Scribner's Sons, 1911), p. 94.

12. Edward Alsworth Ross, *Principles of Sociology* (New York: The Century Company, 1930), p. 112.

13. Wiebe, *The Search for Order: 1877–1920*, pp. 2–3.

14. Richard P. Taub with Doris L. Taub, eds., *American Society: In Tocqueville's Time and Today* (Chicago: Rand McNally College Publishing Co., 1974), p. 78.

15. Robert E. Park, Ernest W. Burgess, and Roderick D. McKenzie, *The City* (Chicago: University of Chicago Press, 1925), pp. 71–72.

16. Bert E. Swanson, *The Concern for Community in Urban America* (New York: Odyssey Press, 1970), p. 112.

17. Louis Wirth, *On Cities and Social Life*, Albert J. Reiss, Jr., ed. (Chicago: University of Chicago Press, 1964), p. 63.

18. Robert Ezra Park, *Human Communities: The City and Human Ecology*, Everett Cherrington Hughes et al., eds. (Glencoe, Ill.: The Free Press, 1952), p. 59.

19. Wirth, *On Cities and Social Life*, pp. 70–80.

20. Marion Wesley Roper, "The City and the Primary Group," in *Contributions to Urban Sociology*, Ernest W. Burgess and Donald J. Bogue, eds. (Chicago: University of Chicago Press, 1964), p. 233.

21. Park, Burgess, and McKenzie, *The City*, p. 40.

22. Robert E. Park, *On Social Control and Collective Behavior: Selected Papers*, Ralph H. Turner, ed. (Chicago: University of Chicago Press, 1967), pp. 10–11.

23. Park, *Human Communities: The City and Human Ecology*, p. 80.

24. Cited in Swanson, *The Concern for Community in Urban America*, p. 120.

25. Wirth, *On Cities and Social Life*, p. 82.

26. Cited in a discussion of Emile Durkheim's *The Division of Labor in Society* in Melvin L. DeFleur and Sandra Ball-Rokeach, *Theories of Mass Communication*, 4th ed. (New York: Longman, 1982), p. 156.

27. Orrin E. Klapp, "Style Rebellion and Identity Crisis," in *Human Nature and Collective Behavior: Papers in Honor of Herbert Blumer*, Tamotsu Shibutani, ed. (Englewood Cliffs, N.J.: Prentice-Hall, Inc., 1970), pp. 77–78.

28. Nisbet, *Community and Power*, p. 7.

29. Edward E. Lawler III, *Motivation in Work Organizations* (Monterey, Calif.: Brooks/Cole Publishing Co., 1973), p. 209.

30. Nisbet, *Community and Power*, p. 52.

31. Ibid., p. 11.

32. Swanson, *The Concern for Community in Urban America*, p. 105.

33. William E. Francois, *Introduction to Mass Communications and Mass Media* (Columbus, Ohio: Grid, Inc., 1977), p. 57.

34. DeFleur and Ball-Rokeach, *Theories of Mass Communication*, p. 157.

35. Klapp, "Style Rebellion and Identity Crisis," pp. 78–79.

36. Ibid., p. 79.

37. Belman, "The Idea of Communication in the Social Thought of the Chicago School," pp. 2–3.

38. Jean B. Quandt, *From the Small Town to the Great Community: The Social Thought of Progressive Intellectuals* (New Brunswick, N.J.: Rutgers University Press, 1970), p. 17.

39. Ernest W. Burgess, *On Community, Family, and Delinquency*, Leonard S. Cottrell, Jr. et al., eds. (Chicago: University of Chicago Press, 1973), pp. 18–19.

40. Etymologically instructive is Williams's reminder that "society" once referred to active fellowship, company, or a common way of doing things, while the term is now used to describe a general system or order. Likewise, "individual" once meant indivisible, a member of the group; now it has the meaning of separateness and even of opposition. See Raymond Williams, *Marxism and Literature* (Oxford: Oxford University Press, 1977), pp. 11–12.

41. Burgess, *On Community, Family, and Delinquency*, pp. 18–19.

42. Francois, *Introduction to Mass Communications and Mass Media*, p. 52.

43. John Dewey, *Democracy and Education: An Introduction to the Philosophy of Education* (New York: The Macmillan Co., 1916), p. 29.

44. Charlotte Jones, "Homelessness in Modern Society: Mead, Berger and Mass Communication," *The Journal of Communication Inquiry* 6 (Summer 1980): 20.

45. George Herbert Mead, *Selected Writings*, Andrew J. Reck, ed. (Indianapolis: Bobbs-Merrill Co., Inc., 1964), pp. 365–366.

46. Park, *Human Communities: The City and Human Ecology*, p. 66.

47. Ibid., p. 181.

48. Ibid., p. 182.

49. Introduction by Ralph H. Turner in Park, *On Social Control and Collective Behavior: Selected Papers*, p. xxviii.

50. Park, *Human Communities: The City and Human Ecology*, p. 66.

51. Park, Burgess, and McKenzie, *The City*, p. 145.

52. Park, *Human Communities: The City and Human Ecology*, p. 58.

53. Robert E. Park and Herbert A. Miller, *Old World Traits Trans-*

planted (New York: Arno Press and The New York Times, 1969), pp. 270–271.

54. Park, Burgess, and McKenzie, *The City*, p. 104.

55. Ibid., p. 65.

56. Ibid., p. 105.

57. George H. Mead, *Mind, Self & Society: From the Standpoint of a Social Behaviorist* (Chicago: University of Chicago Press, 1934), p. 265.

58. Robert Ezra Park, *Race and Culture* (Glencoe, Ill.: The Free Press, 1950), p. 42.

59. Mead, *Selected Writings*, p. 369.

60. Robert E. Park and Ernest W. Burgess, *Introduction to the Science of Sociology: Including the Original Index to Basic Sociological Concepts*, 3rd ed., rev. (Chicago: University of Chicago Press, 1969), p. 26.

61. John Dewey, *Intelligence in the Modern World: John Dewey's Philosophy*, Joseph Ratner, ed. (New York: Random House, The Modern Library, 1939), p. 387.

62. Mead, *Mind, Self & Society: From the Standpoint of a Social Behaviorist*, p. 256.

63. Ibid., pp. 267–268.

64. Wirth, *On Cities and Social Life*, p. 70.

65. John Dewey, *The Public and Its Problems* (New York: Henry Holt and Co., 1927), p. 213.

66. Introduction by Joe R. Burnett in *John Dewey: The Middle Works, 1899–1924*, Vol. I: *1899–1901*, Jo Ann Boydston, ed. (Carbondale and Edwardsville: Southern Illinois University Press, 1976), pp. xx-xxi.

67. James W. Carey, "Canadian Communication Theory: Extensions and Interpretations of Harold Innis," in *Studies in Canadian Communications*, Gertrude Joch Robinson and Donald F. Theall, eds. (Montreal: McGill University, 1975), p. 51.

68. Charles Horton Cooley, *Social Process* (Carbondale and Edwardsville: Southern Illinois University Press, 1966), pp. 74–75.

69. Cited in Fred H. Matthews, *Quest for an American Sociology: Robert E. Park and the Chicago School* (Montreal: McGill-Queen's University Press, 1977), p. 192.

70. Park, Burgess, and McKenzie, *The City*, pp. 116–117.

71. Ibid., p. 7.

72. Ibid., p. 84.

73. Quandt, *From the Small Town to the Great Community: The Social Thought of Progressive Intellectuals*, pp. 48–49.

74. John Dewey, *Art as Experience* (New York: Capricorn Books, 1958), p. 244.

75. Park, Burgess, and McKenzie, *The City*, p. 111.

76. Ibid., p. 112.

77. John Dewey, *Experience and Nature* (New York: W. W. Norton & Co., Inc., 1929), p. 202.

78. Ibid., pp. 204–205.

79. Ibid., p. 183.

80. Quandt, *From the Small Town to the Great Community: The Social Thought of Progressive Intellectuals*, pp. 49–50.

81. Park, Burgess, and McKenzie, *The City*, p. 39.

82. Mead, *Mind, Self & Society: From the Standpoint of a Social Behaviorist*, p. 257.

83. Cooley, *Social Organization: A Study of the Larger Mind*, p. 85.

84. Dewey, *The Public and Its Problems*, p. 218.

85. Quandt, *From the Small Town to the Great Community: The Social Thought of Progressive Intellectuals*, p. 75.

86. James W. Carey, "Culture, Geography, and Communications: The Work of Harold Innis in an American Context," in *Culture, Communication, and Dependency: The Tradition of H. A. Innis*, W. H. Melody, L. Salter, and P. Heyer, eds. (Norwood, N.J.: Ablex Publishing Corp., 1981), p. 74.

87. James W. Carey, "A Cultural Approach to Communication," *Communication* 2 (1975): 20.

88. Charles Horton Cooley, *Sociological Theory and Social Research* (New York: Henry Holt and Co., 1930), pp. 290–291.

89. Park, *On Social Control and Collective Behavior: Selected Papers*, p. 34.

90. Ibid., p. 36.

91. Lewis A. Coser, *Masters of Sociological Thought: Ideas in Historical and Social Context*, 2nd ed. (San Diego: Harcourt Brace Jovanovich, 1977), pp. 312–313.

92. Dewey, *The Public and Its Problems*, p. 219.

93. Alexis de Tocqueville, *Democracy in America*, Richard D. Heffner, ed. (New York: Mentor Books, 1956), p. 203.

94. Introduction by Robert E. Park in Helen MacGill Hughes, *News and the Human Interest Story* (Chicago: University of Chicago Press, 1940; reprint ed., New Brunswick, N.J.: Transaction Books, 1981), 8th page among unnumbered pages.

95. Park, *Race and Culture*, pp. 22–23.

PART III
A CASE STUDY
RECONCILING
PUBLIC RELATIONS
AND COMMUNITY

We have never excluded people, but, at the same time, we don't
like people coming down and telling us what to do.

Sugar Creek Resident

11
A Review of the Main Theory

Attitudes of U.S. business toward the public have changed greatly since the robber baron era of the late nineteenth and early twentieth centuries. With the growth of an increasingly complex society came the creation of numerous and varied publics. Business found that it had to identify these publics and take them into account. Furthermore, the publics were to hold business, as well as all other organizations, accountable for their actions. The primary responsibility to maintain relations and to resolve problems with their publics became the task of public relations practitioners.

Some historians say that the roots of public relations can be traced to the dawn of civilization. But, they argue, it was the era of early nineteenth century press-agentry up until the time of business's excesses during the post-Civil War reconstruction period that brought forth the turn-of-the-century origins of modern public relations. The field has been expanding ever since.

As many scholars describe the evolution of public relations and as most professionals perform their jobs, modern public relations practice can probably best be defined as a vocation utilizing persuasive communication to obtain a vested goal on behalf of a represented client. Such a description of public relations today does not seem adequate. The description is narrow and technical and fails to take sufficient account of public relations' role in society. Public relations historians, by and large, have not recognized and appreciated many of the underlying reasons why public relations evolved or the reasons why public relations expanded and emerged as an essential component in society. The result has been diffused and confused thinking about the field.

Contemporary definitions of public relations demonstrate the lack of overall precision in its practice, and today's practitioners are unable to provide an adequate and specific description of the public relations function. These concerns raise critical questions: Does the history of public relations as it is commonly presented adequately or even accurately describe why public relations exists today? What is an appropriate definition of public relations, its role and function?

If the term "public relations" is so broad and ill-defined as to be meaningless, "community relations" also is inadequate for the same reasons. Further, the concept of "community" as used in community relations literature is a misnomer. Public relations practitioners do not practice community relations. They are simply utilizing persuasive communication to obtain specified goals for their clients, and these goals are directed toward a geographic public.

In short, the present level of understanding and explanation of public relations as a professional endeavor is deficient. But this deficiency can be useful in searching for a more suitable definition, role, and function of public relations. Many of the social and organizational ills that thoughtful public relations practitioners voice concern about, but do not directly address, first occurred at the approximate time that modern public relations evolved, namely, from about 1890 to World War I. Social upheavals of the time shattered the public sense of community. New means of communication and transportation were two of the main culprits. Modern public relations—which often justifies its role and function, in part, because of the deficiencies of contemporary society—does not address itself specifically to the problem of restoration and maintenance of community.

Our argument is that an appropriate approach to community

relations should be an active and direct attempt to restore and maintain a sense of community. Only through such a conceptual approach does the practice of community relations deal directly with the problems shared by the organization and its geographic public.

Such an approach, however, requires practitioners to view community relations and its role and function from another perspective, one with a deeper philosophical base and a more abstract outlook. This perspective, to a large extent, has to be independent of the existing literature of public relations, which does not present an adequate history to allow practitioners to understand the need for public relations and which does not define public relations and its role and function in a way that permits adequate and appropriate consideration of both organizational and societal problems.

The perspective we offer of community relations comes from the theoretical work of the Chicago School of Social Thought. Public relations literature makes limited use of a few of the concepts of the Chicago School. Yet much of what the school had to say seems directly relevant to community relations as it could be practiced with an overall goal of restoration and maintenance of community.

Practitioners do not sufficiently appreciate that in a modern mass society the individual has become a homogeneous, segmented, and deeply private individual, alienated from others. Practitioners do not recognize that this was directly caused by the advent of modern means of communication and transportation, which nationalized and resegmentized U.S. society and inverted the relationship between public and private life. Together with the resultant trend toward urban living, these communication and transportation systems caused a loss of community, which has created many social problems affecting both the practitioners' organizations and society.

Practitioners fail to recognize that this loss of community has contributed to the evolution of contemporary public relations. We believe that, through attempts by public relations practitioners to help restore and maintain a sense of community, many of the public relations problems that today's practitioners concern themselves with would not have occurred or would be resolved more easily and satisfactorily within an environment imbued with a strong sense of community.

While this may not negate many traditional strategies, tactics, and activities of contemporary public relations practitioners, it does require a radical change of perspective, a different theoretical base, and an understanding of the causes of the societal ills that plague contemporary society. As a facilitator of communication—ritual communication in a broad sense— public relations practitioners should take a preemptory role in building a sense of community among members of the organization and the geographic public.

Community relations, to best serve its function, must offer more than a superficial combination of assuring a good environment for the organization, more than a simplistic concern for altruistic good citizenship, and more than mere emphasis on the techniques of community involvement. Rather, it must carry out its role from a justifiable theoretical rationale that supports an active attempt at restoration and maintenance of community.

12
Sugar Creek as a Theory Test Site

It is one thing to talk theory. And another to put it to the test. We wanted to see how the communication theories focusing on sense of community as embodied in the Chicago School of Social Thought stood up in a real-world setting. We wanted an approach that would take into account historical factors and at the same time permit the consideration of those nuances and unexpected events that so often are the victims of stringent research design. We chose to carry out a case study, that is, to examine one company's public and community relations programs in the context of one community. More specifically, the method could be characterized as qualitative or, still more specifically, as dealing with natural or life history. Some explanation of these methodological approaches is in order.

The case study is familiar to most public relations practitioners. The approach, as noted by Severin and Tankard, enables an investigator to examine multiple characteristics of a subject—as compared, say, to survey research, which examines fewer characteristics of many subjects.[1] The strength of the case method is the opportunity to study a subject uninhibitedly and in depth.

Qualitative research has come to describe a variety of social scientific methods, which can be differentiated from so-called quantitative research, or physical science methods. Historical in design, qualitative research, according to Christians and Carey,[2] concerns itself with concepts that yield meaningful portraits and not statistically precise formulations derived from artificial conditions. To elaborate:

> The social scientist must study the human spirit as expressed through symbolic imagery. "The Chicago School" taught us that social feelings (attitudes and sentiments) and life-style are most fully expressed in actual situations, and must be recovered unobtrusively through participant observation, from personal documents, and by open-ended interviewing. To get inside the realm of lived experience, the natural processes of communication are especially valuable (such as correspondence, eyewitness accounts, songs, jokes, folklore, memoranda, diaries, ceremonies, citizen group reports, sermons), and methods must be avoided that disrupt the social process and thereby skew our vision.[3]

Natural history was the principal method of inquiry of Chicago School scholar Park. He held that natural history was a typical or collective account of events, the sequence of which leads to establishment of a form rather than a specific instance.[4] Life history is a similar approach, depending heavily on the historical and the descriptive and emphasizing personal communication sources. Life history data serve as a means to make preliminary explorations and orientations in relation to specific research problems, according to Burgess and Bogue.[5] Such data also afford opportunities for theory-building through the formulation of hypotheses for subsequent study.

Our method might be described as life history. It allowed indepth exploration of a city and organization in a way that was relatively free of prior assumptions and that would allow ample opportunity for discovery.

Our information sources included extensive on-site personal interviews with Sugar Creek, Missouri, community officials and residents as well as with Standard Oil (now Amoco) Company officials both at the Sugar Creek test site and at corporate and regional headquarters. Also providing primary data were newspaper archives reporting on the life and ultimate death of the oil refinery in Sugar Creek as well as personal and organizational documents, including correspondence. One of the authors visited the city and area frequently over a period of about seven months in 1982. Underlying the actual data collection was a heightened concern on the part of the investigators for that evanescent yet identifiable quality called community.

From the outset we realized that probably no ideal site existed for our purposes. This is always the problem when reconciling theory and practice. But, as Rousseau—writing about government—put it, it is good logic to reason from the actual to the possible.[6] We finally settled on Sugar Creek, Missouri, as a test site. An Amoco refinery was located there. The city seemed to be the antithesis of what modern mass society is today. Sugar Creek appeared to be an eighteenth century village amid the urban sprawl of cosmopolitan and metropolitan Kansas City. Sugar Creek, its refinery, and the people of Sugar Creek seemed to have existed for more than three-quarters of a century as a true community, much as in the manner espoused by the Chicago School.

Historical evidence points toward Sugar Creek as being an unusual city in contemporary mass society, one where a sense of community has always been, in fact, highly evident. The refinery, the city, and the people of Sugar Creek experienced the same changes that most Americans experienced with the advent of modern mass society. But for a variety of reasons, these changes were not nearly so pronounced. Important for our purposes, the refinery, through a program of community relations, helped to foster this sense of community that the people of Sugar Creek have, to a great extent, maintained.

To understand Sugar Creek, one must know something about Standard Oil Company and the companies it parented. It is ironic that John D. Rockefeller gave $10 million in 1891 from his Standard Oil Company profits to found the University of Chicago and then supported it generously afterward.[7] The university, in turn, became the intellectual center of the Chicago School of Social Thought. Therefore, the school's concerns were partly the consequence of what Rockefeller and other industrialists of his era helped create.

Rockefeller, as a young businessman in Cleveland, had done well dealing in grains, meats, and other products from the

West. In the fall of 1859, word arrived in Cleveland that an oil well at Titusville in western Pennsylvania was producing daily more than 300 gallons of oil worth 50 cents a gallon.[8] Some of Rockefeller's Cleveland acquaintances rushed to the site. Boorstin speculates Rockefeller himself may have made the trip. By 1863, Rockefeller had bought into a Cleveland refinery, and by late 1865 that refinery grossed more than twice as much money ($1.2 million) as any other refinery in the region. Within a generation after the discovery of the well in Titusville, however, the oil industry seemed to be dying. Production went into an uninterrupted decline. Experts became convinced that no further usable supplies of crude oil could be found elsewhere. Then occurred the accidental discovery of a great oil field near Lima, Ohio, in 1885, which, while rich in light products such as benzine and naphtha, had an overpowering odor. Because the oil was so high in sulfur content, it was known as "skunk oil." No known refining method could remove its odor.

Over the protests of his business associates, Rockefeller— already in the oil business—insisted on buying all the Ohio crude oil offered for sale. The odor problem was solved by German-born Herman Frasch, experimenting with highly sulfurous Canadian crude. In May 1888 Standard Oil Trust officials bought Frasch's Canadian plant and patents and put him to work at their Cleveland refinery.

Meanwhile, trust officials were dealing with another difficulty. The company had an extensive marketing organization for its refined Pennsylvania oils, but all the kerosene and lubricants for midwestern and western markets had to be shipped from Cleveland or from even further east. To cut freight costs, officers decided to build a major refinery in or near Chicago.[9]

On May 5, 1889, construction began on a refinery in Whiting, Indiana. Less than two months later, papers were filed to incorporate a Standard Oil Company in Indiana to manufacture, transport, and sell products of crude petroleum. The company was paying high wages for those times, and construction work on the refinery went quickly. On September 2, 1890, Whiting's first 600-barrel still was charged with Lima crude. On Thanksgiving Day, the first shipment of kerosene made by the Frasch process left the refinery, and, by the end of that year, Whiting was in a position to refine almost a tenth of the total U.S. production of crude oil. Whiting was the first major refinery west of Cleveland.[10]

Rockefeller was highly successful in the Whiting venture and in many others to come. He was ingenious at playing off competing railroads against one another; he set up his own cooperage plants, bought his own forests to supply the lumber, produced his own chemicals for the refining process, bought ships and railroad cars to carry his products, and found new markets for by-products.[11] He envisioned a huge combine to control the market, and created the Standard Oil Company of Ohio. Already by 1872 his company had become the largest operation of its kind anywhere. Then he went into the pipeline business. By 1890 he had extended his marketing and was using a fleet of tank wagons to deliver kerosene to customers' doors. When the Sherman Antitrust Act of 1890 was passed and the Standard Oil Trust of Ohio was dissolved by that state's supreme court in 1892, Rockefeller's lawyers invented the "holding company."[12] This was a new kind of organization, whose corporate powers implicitly included the power to hold shares of other companies. Such a device was not outlawed by New Jersey's new General Incorporation Act, so the Standard Oil Company of New Jersey was formed in 1899 as a holding company.[13]

On May 15, 1911, the U.S. Supreme Court ruled that Standard Oil of New Jersey was a combination in restraint of trade and must be dissolved under the Sherman Antitrust Act. By the end of that year, Standard of New Jersey had cut its corporate ties with the 33 other Standard Oil companies in the combination. Each of the 33 then became a separate and independent company. A short time later, the companies began competing with one another. However, the Indiana company really changed very little.[14]

The new stills allowed a far greater percentage of gasoline to be distilled, satisfying the increasing demand for gasoline without glutting the market for other oil products.[15] The company grew and prospered. Today the size of Standard Oil Company (Indiana)—renamed Amoco Corporation in 1985—is immense.

Such a large, powerful company could easily dwarf Sugar Creek, the tiny city of about 5,000 population that was created primarily by and for the large company. Near the turn of the century, before the dissolution of Standard Oil of New Jersey in 1911, executives of the Standard Oil organization in New York City watched the declining production of the older oil fields and the sensational new developments in the Southwest. They decided to provide refining facilities for Oklahoma and Kansas oil by building a new refinery near the Mid-Continent field. It would be closer to many of their consumers. Too, they would build a pipeline from the Mid-Continent field to supply Whiting, which had been depending on the declining Lima field for its crude supply. Such a line would connect with the transit line in Chicago, to serve refineries in the East, if necessary.

Standard officials decided to locate the new refinery near Kansas City, Missouri, for several reasons. It was close to the new producing areas, and Kansas City was a large and growing metropolitan area with a railroad center having trunk lines spreading throughout the developing West and Southwest.[16]

In Fall 1903 Whiting officials selected a site three miles north of Independence and about ten miles east of Kansas City, where a break in the bluffs afforded a frontage of about 2,000 feet on the Missouri River. It was well above the high water mark of the flood of 1903 and had possible railroad connections with both the Santa Fe and the Kansas City Southern. The original site consisted of a triangular piece of 120 acres having high hills on two sides and the Santa Fe Railroad and Missouri River on the other side. A small stream called Sugar Creek meandered through the refinery area into the Missouri.[17]

In March 1904 officials from Whiting came to supervise construction. Shops at Whiting turned out all kinds of materials for the Sugar Creek refinery; carloads of iron and other materials were shipped daily.[18] Despite its having rained on 76 of the first 90 days, construction progressed at astonishing speed, and, by October 1904, 30 stills were put into operation. Upon completion, the refinery began supplying Whiting's former trade in Kansas, Nebraska, western Missouri, Iowa, and parts of Oklahoma, Colorado, and Wyoming. By 1906 the refinery had a daily capacity of about 12,000 barrels.[19] In 1911 it became part of Standard Oil Company (Indiana).

An oil refinery usually produces a city, and around this evolved and grew the city of Sugar Creek. The city did not become incorporated until 1920, nearly two decades after completion of the refinery.

Heavily industrialized cities, including refinery towns, usually rank alongside steel towns and coal towns for dirt and pollution. They have the reputation of being rough places. Crime, vice, and corruption often stake a claim. In short, an oil refinery town usually isn't the first place where middle or upper middle class folks want to live.

At first glance, Sugar Creek seemed to fit the stereotype of a rough-and-tumble oil town. To the north and winding northeast was the Missouri River, expansive by the time it passed Sugar Creek. To the west was a seedy part of Independence, poor, urban, industrialized, and adjoining Kansas City. To the south, just across U.S. Highway 24, was more of Independence, a drab and dreary part of that city of more than 100,000. Local residents will tell you that along the stretch of Highway 24 in Independence was where you found the high crime. Rusted pickup trucks, battered cars, and motorcycles dotted the highway. To the east, Sugar Creek adjoined Independence again. It was to the east and north, along the river, where stolen cars—or their remains—were left, and where bodies were dumped from homicides in Kansas City.

Visitors got to Sugar Creek by crossing the long Missouri River bridge from the north on Missouri 291, turning west on Kentucky Road, and proceeding a few miles along the hilly wooded terrain. First they saw the homes of Sugar Creek. Then the refinery. And finally Sterling Avenue, the main street. Or if they approached from U.S. Highway 24 on the south, they turned north at Sterling and saw the green Sugar Creek sign. On a bluff by the river a few miles farther north was the refinery.

The refinery—closed now since 1982—was large, black, and foreboding, with railroad cars by the hundreds and semi-trucks coming and leaving at all hours of the day and night. The town had only one main street, Sterling Avenue, with no retail businesses to speak of except for a few restaurants and taverns. Residential areas were on the hilly, wooded side streets, to the west and east of Sterling.

The refinery dwarfed everything else in Sugar Creek as it sat atop a bluff of the Missouri River and spewed fire from dozens of smokestacks. The fire could be seen for miles, giving to Sugar Creek a visibility that the town itself did not have.

Sugar Creek was always thought of as a refinery town and only that. People in Sugar Creek were called "Creekers," but usually not to their faces. The place wasn't visited much by outsiders.[20]

The town was strongly Democratic and Catholic. Former Mayor R. J. Roper was in office more than 40 years. He was a political boss of the old order and a highly successful businessman, who remembered the old days just after Prohibition when he had to see Kansas City political boss Tom Pendergast personally to be able to begin a beer distribution company. Roper, probably more than anyone else, was an antagonist of the refinery during his long tenure as mayor and was instrumental in bringing to the town most of its improved services and facilities. Yet he was also among the most ardent supporters of the refinery at Sugar Creek and of what the refinery represented.

Sugar Creek may not appear to be the ideal community envisioned by members of the Chicago School in their search for community. Oil refineries, the one in Sugar Creek included, do not lend themselves to pastoralism.

Yet one lifelong resident expressed the sentiments of the majority when he said that Sugar Creek had always been a good place to live and to bring up children. The town had nice parks and a large community swimming pool, and the atmosphere was that of a friendly and family-oriented town. Tax structures and levies were extremely reasonable.

While the typical refinery town may be portrayed as a rough place, Sugar Creek—by all accounts—was a peaceful family town. It was quiet, prosperous, and law-abiding.

But some residents said that it hadn't always been that way. One remembered:

Sugar Creek was a rough town at one time. During the twenties and the depression years. The reason for this was, when the Slovacs and the Croatians came over to this country, they were a proud, but humble, people. They were in a new country. They were cautious, they were looking for something so much better than what they had; they thought they found it here. They were shy, yet proud, and it soon became apparent that they would stand up for what they felt. They would prefer to be left alone, and they didn't like intruders, and when intruders came in, they got rather violent.

But then he added:

There has never been any trouble down here; we have always taken care of our own problems. There is no rough and toughness down here; we won't allow it to happen.

From World War II to 1982, Sugar Creek changed little in terms of community life. Despite being a refinery town with a tough reputation, many activities revolved around the churches. The youth rebellions of the late 1960s and early 1970s reached Sugar Creek. Many young people left. Later, however, there was a visible turnaround, with the younger generation coming back and taking an active part in church and community activities.

We spoke with the parish priest, an outsider, who spoke about differences between Sugar Creek and other cities. He noted that the people of Sugar Creek were great storytellers and kept telling stories about how things were in the "good old days." This was a great community binder, he said. Petty differences persisted among some residents because of the strike at the refinery in 1959, and scabs and strikers still—more than 20 years later—held hard feelings toward one another.

Despite being in a large metropolitan area, Sugar Creek had small town values. Everybody knew everybody else and what they threw into their trash. The priest encountered people he knew everywhere—on the streets, at the ball park. This created a sense of belonging, even though long memories can also include hurt. There was more visiting around than in suburbia.

Sugar Creek children had to go to school outside Sugar Creek.

They competed well and, in fact, excelled, giving outsiders the feeling that the children came from solid families with a sense of worth and dignity. Not many have gone on to become professionals such as lawyers or doctors or teachers. Those who attended college seldom went beyond a bachelor's degree.

Although Sugar Creek was an industrial town next to Kansas City, there was little of the crime characteristic of such an area, and the town remained a residential town. After a social event, folks commonly stopped at a neighborhood—call it "family"—bar for a beer. There may have been an unspoken problem with alcoholism, one resident said, because there was pressure to drink.

Catholicism was dominant but not the only religion. The heavily Democratic town had only one active Republican, but he was well-accepted because he was one of them, a fellow Sugar Creeker.

Because there were few downtown retail stores, people did not see one another shopping except maybe at the Independence Safeway, where a great many people from other areas also shopped. It was in the Sugar Creek taverns and restaurants where Sugar Creekers saw one another.

Sugar Creek was a prosperous town with excellent city services. Residents worried about the refinery's closing in 1982, but the town's attitude was: "We are going to make it because we've got one another."

Much of what has been discussed can perhaps be attributed to the ethnic characteristics of the people who live in Sugar Creek, with or without an oil refinery and with or without an industry with a community relations program. Sugar Creek had two main ethnic groups: The Slovs, who came from Slovakia, a part of south-central Czechoslovakia close to the Austria-Hungary border; and the Croatians, who came from Yugoslavia. These two groups at one time made up 80–90 percent of the city's population. At the time of our study, the percentage was about 40–50. Most of the residents were white.

The strike against the refinery in 1959 changed the complexion of the town forever. Brother was pitted against brother. Residents remembered incidents of relatives being taken into protective custody for violating court injunctions and of having to pick up nails in driveways each morning. The refinery finally broke the strike, but bitter memories lingered.

Despite such hard feelings, it was always recognized that the refinery was good for the town economically. The refinery's closing in 1982 meant the loss of about a half million dollars of tax revenue to the town.

A Standard Oil official who had spent most of his career with the company in community relations said that the company's goal in Sugar Creek had been to promote better relationships with the community. The community relations program began formally in 1952 through the efforts of Conger Reynolds, then public relations director of Standard Oil (Indiana), who was based in Chicago. One way the company carried out its responsibility was to encourage employees to take part in civic affairs. The company also held open houses for school groups, sponsored Christmas parties, and began publishing in 1959 a local employee magazine, the *Reactor*.

The company wanted to be a responsible citizen, according to officials. And residents seemed to think of the corporation as an independent and valued citizen in what they felt strongly was their community.

13

Public and Community Relations in Sugar Creek

During the 75-year relationship between the refinery and the city of Sugar Creek, several distinct periods can be identified. These range from the early years, through what might be called a golden era, and to the eventual dissolution of the refinery not long after it had observed its diamond jubilee in the city of Sugar Creek. Relations between the town and refinery ran the gamut of good to bad. These relations are explored in this chapter.

Rockefeller and his Standard Oil Company were more often than not castigated, but the company officials seemed to have some sense of public relations. Perhaps their idea of public relations, in some respects, was more honest than is often practiced today. In his day, Rockefeller paid the best wages, provided hospital facilities for employees when they were sick, and paid old-age pensions when they retired. This was done in a spirit of benevolent paternalism, to be sure, for he never conceded the employee's right to demand benefits or to organize to obtain benefits.

A ruthless businessman, a generous benefactor to the downtrodden, a stern but benevolent employer—Rockefeller was all of these. Whether these traits were translated into the type of community relations program that his company tried to embrace is debatable. But much of Rockefeller's reputation comes through clearly in stories about the early days of Sugar Creek.

EARLY YEARS—1904–29

It was March 1904 when people from Whiting came to build the refinery, after the site was chosen in 1903. By Fall 1904 the refinery neared completion.[21] The first crude oil arrived at 8 a.m. on October 14, 1904, and eight days later the refinery began operations.[22]

There is little doubt that Sugar Creek began as a product of benevolent paternalism. During the early years the town was under the direct influence of the refinery. Even when it was incorporated in 1920, the town had a mayor who also was a refinery executive.[23] After a boomtown period of a few years with the usual accompanying social problems, the town buckled down in an attempt to become a wholesome family-type city. Despite active attempts by Independence to gain economic and political control over Sugar Creek, the town maintained its own identity and sense of self-reliance.

There was a self-righteous attitude on the part of the Independence business community, as exemplified in the reportage of the *Independence Examiner*—which was one of abhorrence toward what Rockefeller and Standard Oil represented, but one of vested self-interest as far as the Sugar Creek refinery was concerned. While big business could be damned, the refinery at Sugar Creek was just fine, along with the revenue potential it brought.[24] Long before the issue was fashionable, the refinery got into trouble over both air and water pollution. Little was done about the air, but the company actively sought to correct its water pollution problems after being nudged to do so.[25]

The company did some unwise things. For example, in one instance, it did not allow Sugar Creek to use its fire-fighting equipment in time of need.[26] But later, when the Missouri Supreme Court threatened to force the company to leave the state because of questionable financial dealings, people came readily to its defense, again through primarily self-vested motives.[27]

There appear to be no documented instances where the refinery mandated decisions for the city to follow, although it would be naive to assume that this did not occur. The refinery had political clout through its executives and employees who held positions in city government. The refinery also provided most of the tax revenue. Yet there is nothing to indicate that the refinery ever did anything overtly harmful to the city or the citizenry of Sugar Creek.

Indeed, the company seemed to be very conscious of public relations, based on its extensive institutional advertising in newspapers in the late 1910s—which gives (usually from a defensive stance) an idea of what issues it considered important to assure public acceptance. However, none of these advertisements—well-written and strategically presented even by today's standards—dealt directly with community relations, although several touched on the subject. If the concept of community occurred at all in these advertisements, it was primarily as a community of employees, stockholders, and customers.[28] At times, the advertisements seemed hypocritical, for example, mentioning integrity at about the time a company official was failing to answer questions from the Teapot Dome committee.[29] Overall the ads seemed to corroborate that the company was doing a conscientious job of caring for its employees, stockholders, and customers—in a manner highly unusual for the era.

In a rudimentary way, the company did show an understanding of how to create a sense of community. This came about through its active support of baseball leagues, band concerts, picnics, and other events and activities that helped the citizens of Sugar Creek become a community in the true sense of the word and that helped them forge an identity despite an uncommon interest in their activities on the part of the business people and citizens of Independence. No one will know for sure the exact motives of the refinery employees and the refinery-employed city officials in trying to build and improve the services of Sugar Creek during this period. Many residents felt that the refinery did not do nearly enough, although all showed a great appreciation for the refinery's role as the lifeblood of the city.

By the end of the 1920s, Sugar Creek was both a city and a community. Despite its proximity to Independence and Kansas City, it did not become annexed or even a suburb. Rather, it was a definite city with its own unique personality. In a passive sort of way, the refinery fostered and encouraged this sense of community.

INTERMEDIATE YEARS—1930–45

From 1930 through 1945, Sugar Creek and much of the rest of the world experienced difficult times—a Great Depression and a World War. Though the company had hired a public relations director based in Chicago, Standard Oil Company (Indiana) did not seem to do much more in the area of community relations during this time than it had done before. In some ways, it could be argued that it did less. Neverthless, the people of Sugar Creek survived the depression and the war with their lifestyles and values pretty much intact. The relationship with the company remained much the same as before. The exception was a new political machine that took control of the city and was not afraid to become an antagonist to the large company owning the refinery.

In late 1929 Conger Reynolds was appointed director of public relations of the corporation of Standard Oil (Indiana). He believed in the importance of good community relations, and later developed several community relations strategies that remain state-of-the-art.[30] In fact, Conger Reynolds was to become a national pioneer in the practice of public relations for the community.

Despite the appearance of Reynolds at corporate headquarters, the refinery in Sugar Creek seems to have contributed no more to community relations during 1930–45 than it had during the earlier period. No doubt, national problems—the depression-era economy and then the war—made heavy demands on everyone. This may have dampened somewhat the overt concern for community. But this explanation is not completely satisfactory because it could be argued similarly that such uncertain times might heighten the need for sense of community.

Evidence suggests that the sense of community existing since the establishment of the refinery—and hence the start of the town—merely continued during these years. The company appears to have done nothing more by way of promoting community relations than it had done before. Maybe it did even less.

People working at the refinery were grateful for the security and relative prosperity that the refinery provided them and their families during the depression. Some employees had their working hours reduced for a short time but soon returned to a normal workweek. The company spread out the available work to as many people as possible during lean production times.[31]

During this time Sugar Creek remained a fairly close-knit community, and the refinery contributed to this sense of belonging. For example, the company sponsored a week-long celebration on its 31st anniversary of operation and invited the "entire community."[32] Its benevolent paternalism was evident when it bailed out the Sugar Creek State Bank, to the relief of many of its own employees as well as to other residents.[33] The company's annuity plan also was a blessing to Sugar Creek, because it assured security and even prosperity to retired people living there.[34] The company's celebration of its 50th anniversary in 1939 was an event that helped to hold and increase the bond among the people of Sugar Creek themselves and between them and the refinery.[35] Also in 1939, after an explosion at the refinery, the concern and support given to its employees exemplified the company's regard for its workers. The event also revealed that the refinery did not have a clear idea about the advantages of open communication with the press. Officials withheld key information about the explosion—which killed one person and injured three others—resulting in this comment in the July 18, 1939, *Independence Examiner*:

> Due to the air-tight censorship that the Standard Oil Company imposes upon all of its employees, it was impossible to get details in the form of an official statement for some time after the fire started. [An official] when seen at the hospital refused to give any information at all, however he was on the job in the company's interest looking after the injured men.[36]

If Sugar Creek maintained its sense of community during this period, nevertheless there were indications that change was imminent. A new mayor was taking office.[37] As a result, the company was becoming a more cautious, albeit perhaps more responsible, citizen. Also, the expansion of the city of Sugar Creek brought about the first major rift between the refinery—which did not want its newly purchased adjoining property annexed—and the city.[38] This addition of land, which included residential areas, meant that Sugar Creek would no longer be a small village in terms of population, size, and the homogeneity of its citizens. The scene was set for change. What was good for the company was not necessarily good for the community, and vice versa.

GOLDEN YEARS—1946–55

The years 1946 through 1955 brought about the most active community relations effort on the part of the refinery, but not always with satisfactory results. In some ways, the aggressive community relations efforts of the company may have been detrimental to the sense of community at Sugar Creek. Later, after a period of national and international turmoil, Sugar Creek itself would experience violence and strife between the refinery and the community. But not until a kind of golden era had flourished in the life of Sugar Creek from 1946 to 1955.

It might have been assumed that after World War II the community relations program of the refinery would actively seek not only to maintain good relations with Sugar Creek but also to sustain the sense of community that was all but lost almost everywhere else. In earlier years both the refinery and the city seemed to appreciate what they had in Sugar Creek. Indeed, the immense societal changes of the post–World War II era in many respects bypassed Sugar Creek. Labor unrest, return of servicemen, and regearing of the economy for peacetime—together with changed life experiences and values—were among the factors that produced dramatic changes throughout the nation.

Refinery community relations efforts ranged from publicly recognizing employee service and enhancing staff benefits to providing short newsreels to schools. The activities represented state-of-the-art public relations tactics for the time and would hardly be considered obsolete today.

For the refinery and the city the era was one of prosperity with visions of a bright future. But much of what took place did not translate into restoration and maintenance of community. While both the city and the refinery sought to become bigger and supposedly better, there seemed to be much less appreciation of what the community and refinery actually meant to each other. The refinery made it clear, for example, in many of its communication efforts that Sugar Creek was no more important than were Independence, the adjoining suburbs of Kansas City, and the Greater Kansas City metropolitan area itself. Many of the activities of the refinery during this period exemplify the type of community relations that is usually practiced today. A desire to persuade, together with a genuine sense of altruism, provided the main impetus for community relations activities.

Sugar Creek remained a community during this time, but as a vestige of what had been there previously. The community itself seemed to go unappreciated by a city and a refinery bent on joining the rest of the nation in frenzied postwar growth. Neither the city nor the refinery could be blamed. Opportunity for development abounded and was fueled by a blind belief in the benefits of growth. After all, wouldn't relations between the refinery and city stay the same? Or even get better?

Community relations efforts of the refinery certainly did not produce a negative effect insofar as company–town relations were concerned. To the contrary, many projects were successful in achieving specific objectives. But the sense of community that was the legacy of Sugar Creek from the earliest part of its existence seemed to go unappreciated. There appeared to be little motivation to maintain this sense of community, which the refinery and Sugar Creek had cultivated from the outset.

WATERSHED YEARS—1956–60

After World War II, the changes that took place in the company and in refinery management had long-term ramifications for Sugar Creek and its residents. Effects of the changes were not obvious at first, and some would not be evident until after the 1960s.

After the war, the company had expanded greatly through modernization and improvement of existing refineries. In 1954 American Oil became a wholly-owned subsidiary of Indiana Standard. New parent management took over, and on February 1, 1957, an extensive corporate reorganization took place.[39] Despite the departure of several key corporate public relations officials, including Conger Reynolds (who retired), little change seemed in store for Sugar Creek.[40]

A full-page company advertisement, a "Report to Our Neighbors," in the February 14, 1956, *Independence Examiner*, said, in part:

> We like to believe that our company has contributed to the overall progress of better, easier, more comfortable living that you enjoy today.... Your patronage, friendliness and support have made our progress possible. By continuing safe, stable operations in the Sugar Creek neighborhood, and by bringing you always the finest of petroleum products, we shall try to contribute toward your progress.[41]

The *Kansas City Star* featured Sugar Creek in a series about "suburbs" of Kansas City, noting it was said in the old days that "you have to whip the whole town to get out." The refinery, it pointed out, accounted for more than $5.5 million of Sugar Creek's assessed valuation of $7.25 million, thus providing 80 percent of the tax revenue. But the newspaper also referred to the open break in town and refinery relations over annexation issues.[42]

In 1957, during an "Oil Progress Week" program sponsored by the Independence Chamber of Commerce, a clergyman said he believed that "the refinery is not only in business to find oil and to make good products and to sell them at fair prices; but also the leaders have a deep concern for human relations and deep interest in the welfare of the individual employee." At the same time a company official commented that "a large corporation can have a stout heart and be concerned for the spiritual as well as the material welfare of its employees."[43]

Through its local philanthropy and concern for employees, the company was apparently enjoying the rewards that come from an aggressive and extensive community relations program. Although annexation and taxation disputes continued to test relations between the refinery and Sugar Creek and surrounding Jackson County, the refinery's monthly newsletter commented, "At Sugar Creek we feel good business citizenship goes far beyond providing just a payroll for a community. It means active participation in community, civic and church affairs."[44]

A few days later, on July 8, 1959, a strike began, appearing to be little more than the other short and relatively rare strikes that had hit the plant during its 55 years of operation.[45] But that was not actually the case. The strike lasted eight months.[46] Key issues were seniority and arbitration procedures. Violence erupted, and the economic impact was devastating. After the eleventh week, the refinery estimated that more than $1 million in payroll had been lost by the striking workers.[47] The *Kansas City Star*, noting that the strike had begun calmly enough, then commented, "It is a different story now. Brother has turned against brother, because one has chosen to go back to work and the other is still on strike."[48]

In many respects, the refinery attempted to maintain business as usual. But everybody was relieved when, at 11 p.m. on Friday, March 4, 1960, the refinery found its gates free of pickets for the first time in 241 days. Surprisingly, by the time the strike ended, the refinery had gradually increased operations to about 83 percent of crude capacity using supervisory, professional, technical, and clerical employees, together with the more than 200 union members who had returned to work by that time. Many of the other strikers now found that they had no jobs to return to. The company said that there just weren't as many jobs to go around. Reasons included more efficient refinery operations tested during the strike and an industry-wide oversupply.[49]

Some things remained the same during these years of upheaval. The refinery counseled one of the Greater Kansas City Junior Achievement companies.[50] The United Campaign Committee at the refinery met.[51] About 500 delegates attending the

Future Farmers of America convention in Kansas City toured the plant.[52] And once again officials lit up the 16-story "cat converter" (the fluid catalytic unit—tallest structure at the refinery) as a "Christmas tree" for the holiday season.[53]

But the relationship between the refinery and Sugar Creek would never be the same. And it wasn't the people of the city against the refinery. The strike had divided the city and its residents.

PRELUDE TO THE END—1961–69

The 1960s, although calmer for the refinery and the city of Sugar Creek than was the preceding period, were a prelude to still more massive change. In January 1961 the refinery became an operation of the American Oil Company instead of the Standard Oil Company (Indiana), which became the parent company. Joining the restructuring was Utah Oil Refining Company. The Sugar Creek refinery now became one of 12 refineries in American Oil.[54] A month later nearly 42,000 readers nationwide began receiving a new magazine, *Torch and Oval*, published in Chicago and representing the consolidation of the three major oil companies.[55]

After the debilitating strike and the consolidation, Sugar Creek and the refinery attempted to return to a state of normalcy—whatever that was, anymore. Refinery officials continued many of their public relations efforts, including gifts to charitable organizations, sponsoring of youth programs, and participation in civic affairs. A half-page advertisement in the February 28, 1961, *Independence Examiner* listed the chief products (including gasolines, distillates, residual fuels, asphalt, jet fuels, and petroleum coke) shipped from Sugar Creek and asserted, "Your Sugar Creek Refinery Has Set the Pace in the Oil Industry for the Past 57 Years, 1904–1961."[56]

Meanwhile, in 1964 Standard Oil Company (Indiana) was preparing to observe its 75th anniversary. The *Kansas City Star* noted that there was little fanfare in Sugar Creek.[57] In 1964 the refinery also observed its 60th year of operation, and the city of Sugar Creek adopted a congratulatory resolution.[58]

The refinery, further adjusting to the impact of new technology, reduced its number of employees. At the same time, it was coming under increasing criticism for pollution. Government officials claimed that the pollution ranged from black soot in the air to petroleum wastes in a nearby creek. Company officials were responsive to the complaints and even gained favorable attention for refinery efforts to solve the problems, despite recurrent leaks and odors.[59]

The years had taken their toll, both on Sugar Creek and the refinery. Growth after World War II had meant material prosperity for town and company. Much of the past had vanished. While the refinery and Sugar Creek were larger, fewer Sugar Creek residents were deriving their livelihood from the refinery and, perhaps more significantly, fewer refinery employees were living in Sugar Creek.

The refinery became more impersonal. It became automated with fewer employees, and these employees were often highly skilled individuals who were transferred in and out. Short-term managers became the norm, a radical change from the time when officials held positions for many years. Ruptured relations persisted from the strike.

The corporate name change indicated to the people of Sugar Creek that the company itself was changing. It was easier to criticize a refinery that no longer was an integral part of the community.

END OF A RELATIONSHIP—1970–82

As the city of Sugar Creek and the refinery began the decade of the 1970s, air pollution became an increasing concern and a source of increasing tension. In 1970 the *Independence Observer* praised the efforts of the refinery in installing pollution-reducing systems during the past ten years.[60] But the resolution of one pollution problem seemed to mark the appearance of another.

In January 1971 a new clean air unit began removing about 80 tons of sulphur a day from fuel oil components and refinery gases. The unit was constructed as part of a nationwide program by the oil company and was costing $2 million per month nationally to maintain.[61] In March 1978 the Environmental

Protection Agency asked the Justice Department to file criminal charges against Amoco Oil Company for not properly reporting an oil spill at its Sugar Creek refinery.[62] In 1978 the refinery agreed to install about $15.2 million in odor-reducing air pollution control equipment after the Missouri Air Conservation Commission modified a 1977 air pollution abatement order to require the company to take several major steps toward reducing odor emissions.[63]

Pollution was not the only problem. The refinery's relationship with the city of Sugar Creek—and the city's own existence—became fraught with controversy and occasional hostility over other issues as well, including recurring disputes over tax assessment. Psychologically the company seemed no longer a part of Sugar Creek. And in 1973 the refinery got a new name for the second time in its 68-year history. The corporate name of the company managing the refinery was changed to Amoco Oil Company, from the American Oil Company. Executives said that the change to Amoco followed a corporate trend of the company's parent, Standard Oil Company (Indiana)—which was renamed Amoco Corporation in 1985—to simplify and clarify communications with customers and other members of the public.[64]

It was in 1974 that the lengthy tax assessment battle was resolved. The company protested its 1971, 1972, and 1973 tax assessments after the Missouri Tax Commission had raised the refinery's assessment from $12 million in 1970 to $15.8 million in 1971. Under terms of the settlement, the real estate assessment would be $15 million for each of the four years 1971–74.[65]

The end of the decade ironically brought about a renewed interest among Sugar Creek residents in some of the values and the sense of community that the city and the refinery had enjoyed from the beginning of their relationship. The more turbulent previous decades—to a great extent beginning with the tragic strike in 1959—did not have to mean permanent change or the loss of old values, Sugar Creek residents began to realize.

In 1979, after the refinery and Sugar Creek had coexisted for 75 years, a renewed effort was made to help Sugar Creek strengthen its sense of community. Many of the 2–3,000 families of Sugar Creek began meeting periodically in the basement of St. Cyril's Catholic Church to tape-record anecdotes of older residents, before such stories would be lost forever. The residents were aided by a $300 grant through a Kansas City area ethnic cultural program designed to encourage the metropolitan area's major ethnic groups to study and preserve their heritages.[66]

The decade of the 1980s saw two major changes take place in the life of Sugar Creek. In Spring 1981 Mayor R. J. Roper, who had held that office for 40 years, announced that he would not seek re-election. It was the end of an era. The *Independence Examiner* of May 3, 1981, cited the retiring mayor's numerous accomplishments for the community and commented, "During the 40 years his interest in the welfare of his community has never lagged."[67]

A year later the other shoe dropped. The refinery would be closed as of June 1, 1982. (Actual closing time was slightly later.) The impact of the closing was not so great as many had suspected it would be. Few of the remaining 480 plant employees lived in Sugar Creek. Thus, the loss of the $19 million payroll would be spread around. However, the $300,000 in real estate taxes paid by Amoco, out of $1.5 million the refinery paid each year in state and local taxes, amounted to more than half the real property taxes paid in Sugar Creek.[68]

Sugar Creek's was the third refinery within a year to be closed in the Amoco system due to decreasing revenue resulting from declining demand.[69] On March 5, 1982, the *Kansas City Times* eulogized: "Together the refinery and the town have shared growth and setbacks, storms and accidents and—until now—pinched economic times."[70]

Sugar Creek residents admitted that it would be hard to imagine the town of nearly 4,300 people without the refinery. Many likened the refinery's closing to a death in the family.[71]

14

Lessons from the Chicago School and Sugar Creek

The quest of this book has been for a definition and an approach to public relations that more satisfactorily explain the role of public relations than does existing literature.

The arguments that have evolved are threefold and closely interrelated:

1. An appropriate approach to practicing community (and public) relations must be derived through an active attempt to restore and maintain the sense of community that has been lost in contemporary society.

2. Through attempts by the public relations practitioner to help restore and maintain community, many of the community relations problems that practitioners now concern themselves with would not have evolved or would be more easily resolvable.

3. To attempt to do this requires practitioners to view public relations and its function from another perspective.

Such assertions go against the grain of much current public relations literature and most public relations practice. We do not maintain that public relations practitioners must cast aside their roles as persuaders and advocates, although these activities would be tempered considerably. Neither are the restoration and maintenance of a sense of community offered as a panacea for all public relations problems confronting the practitioner. However, while first appearances indicate that what we advocate would be a roundabout way to creating good community relations, we argue that this is, in fact, the most direct way. Many of the problems that public relations practitioners concern themselves with in modern mass society stem directly from the loss of community.

The Chicago School devoted much of its attention to exploring the underlying reasons for loss of community and suggested ways to restore it. Communication was their focal point. The Chicago School viewed community as necessary to a healthy social structure. The concepts of community and communication were closely related.

The public relations practitioner should heed this relationship. The public relations practitioner's role as a communicator, and more specifically as a communication facilitator, should be his or her highest calling. Being a facilitator of communication in the traditional sense—that is, seeking out and promoting discourse along all avenues—is a role of critical importance today, which can help to build a sense of community among organizations and their geographic publics.

Applying what the Chicago School advocated, and supported by the historical case study, the public relations practitioner can help to restore and maintain a sense of community in several ways. Specifically, we would point to eight:

1. Practitioners can help community members and the organizations they represent become conscious of common interests that are the basis for both their contentions and their solutions. With conscientious thought, practitioners can help citizens in the community maintain their individuality as well as their solidarity.

The case study illustrates that the refinery did this to a considerable extent, often without purposely doing so. In its early history, the benevolently paternalistic refinery gave its primary attention to the small village of Sugar Creek and its people, giving them a place to work, a place to live, a place to play, and a place to form associations—all in an environment that allowed people to form and be conscious of common interests. The refinery, the city, and the people were one in this respect.

As the refinery and the city grew, this consciousness of common interests was threatened, but was never really destroyed. What threatened it was the increasing size of the refinery and the city, with an increased heterogeneity in both, together with a damaging strike, increased automation, and high management turnover at the refinery.

It could be argued from the case study that the refinery really encouraged more of a sense of community earlier in its history than later when "professional" or overt "community relations" efforts were made. In truth, the on-site community relations representatives did raise a consciousness of common interests, although at times they did not fully appreciate that Sugar Creek, not the surrounding metropolitan Kansas City area, was the refinery's real community. The refinery throughout its history, in fact, did encourage a consciousness of common interests, which helped to maintain a sense of community in Sugar Creek. It did this, by and large, with personnel who were not specifically trained in public relations.

2. Practitioners can help individuals in the community to overcome alienation in its several forms. They can help individuals accommodate themselves to the larger group of the community. Practitioners can help members of the community to know one another. They can help develop person-to-person relationships within the community and help community members share personal experiences among one another in a true spirit of community.

This too the refinery did quite well, at first perhaps as a natural result of being the sole major industry in the city. It did foster relationships among the workers, their families, and others in Sugar Creek, a small city where most people worked at the refinery or had a family member who worked there or had some other direct relationship with the refinery. The refinery, the city, and the people were one in their work lives, their social lives, and their family lives. The refinery encouraged this relationship throughout its history. The refinery became a pioneer in the use of community relations personnel, who actively sought to have the refinery continue to be part of the city and the city continue to be part of the refinery. If the community relations personnel seemed at times to want to encompass all of the Kansas City metropolitan area, it was not to the exclusion of Sugar Creek itself, although the latter did not get sufficient attention at times. The people of Sugar Creek could and did become part of Sugar Creek and part of the refinery, knowing one another in a way characteristic of an old social order. The refinery from its earliest days made sincere attempts to integrate the organization, its employees, and Sugar Creek, often through direct attempts at communication and communication facilitation. The efforts were remarkably successful.

3. Practitioners can help their organizations assume the role that Dewey reserved for the public schools, that is, in helping to create a sense of community. Application of new communication technologies—together with an appropriate theoretical understanding of their use—is one way that public relations practitioners can help to fulfill such goals.

The refinery performed this function as well as any school could have. The refinery was involved in all community activities and touched the lives of all the people of Sugar Creek, regardless of whether they worked at the refinery or not. For much of its history the refinery communicated well with the people, although it may not have facilitated communication as well among members of the community during the later periods. The refinery's communication efforts tended to be less successful as the refinery grew, as it hired more people from outside Sugar Creek, as the ravages of the strike caused wounds that would not easily heal, and as automation and turnover of management occurred. The intimacy and fellowship of the refinery and community in earlier days could not be easily replaced by employee magazines, open houses, tours, speaking engagements, and similar efforts. Nevertheless, the efforts of the community relations personnel often were remarkably successful, and their insights into community relations problems were likewise remarkably accurate.

4. Leisure time of contemporary society is not well considered by most organizations. Public relations practitioners should be

cognizant of this and encourage leisure-time activities of citizens to enhance their sense of community.

The refinery responded effectively in this area throughout its history. The activities it sponsored or promoted changed over the years. Whether it was sponsoring ball games and band concerts or participating in Fourth of July parades, the company did consider the leisure time of its employees and the people of Sugar Creek. It was making major contributions in this area at a time when such efforts were highly unusual among businesses. Much of the life of the community revolved around work and leisure as it was provided by the refinery and the environment that the refinery had established.

5. Consummatory, that is, self-fulfilling, communication offers an immediate enhancement of life, which can be enjoyed for its own sake. Most practitioners, concerned with persuasion and advocacy, do not encourage such communication; rather, they focus on merely instrumental, or practical, communication.

A benevolently paternalistic management in the early years of the refinery and, in later years, community relations personnel with little or no formal training in public relations did remarkably well throughout the refinery's history in offering consummatory communication to the employees and to other people in Sugar Creek. It could be argued that such managers and community relations personnel did a better job in this area than public relations personnel schooled in state-of-the-art public relations techniques and with an overt interest in advocacy and persuasion. In much of the communication from the refinery and throughout the refinery, there was evidence of a joy of communication for communication's own sake, which appears to have fostered a sense of community between the refinery and the people of the city.

6. Practitioners can help individuals find security and protection through association with others. Practitioners can help members of the community develop and fulfull their social roles. Practitioners can lead their organizations in charitable works and concern for people within the community.

The refinery was generally benevolent and charitable. There

were notable exceptions. One occurred early in the refinery's history when it would not lend Sugar Creek its fire-fighting equipment. Another took place in the late 1950s when the refinery essentially broke the striking union. Overall, however, the refinery demonstrated throughout its history that charity could take place in a variety of ways, such as bailing out a depression-era bank and making sizable contributions to the Independence sanitarium. The refinery seemed to recognize that employees could not only fulfill a place in the organization but also a place in the community. Much encouragement was given to employees to serve the community in whatever ways the employees felt most appropriate, such as serving in government, taking over classes for teachers, or driving needy children to distant locations for health care. The refinery time and again encouraged the sense of community and charity that was an inherent part of Sugar Creek.

7. Interest in community welfare, social order, and progess can be addressed by public relations practitioners. As a social center, through a concern for art and a concern for community play, the organization can help to enhance community. Practitioners can help the community share aesthetic experience, religious ideas, personal values, and sentiments.

This is not to imply that the organization should project its dominant values onto the community. Rather, the organization should respect and promote opportunities for members of the community to realize and appreciate their own culture. The refinery throughout its history served as a community social center and demonstrated a concern for community play in a broad context. It fostered aesthetic experiences in a variety of ways and showed concern for personal values and sentiments. The refinery did this throughout its history, sometimes actively and sometimes passively, but in a way that represented a significant contribution to the community.

8. Practitioners can help foster personal friendships. They can help individuals to root themselves in the community, to grow with it, gaining in depth, significance, flavor, and absorbing the local tradition and spirit.

The refinery certainly contributed to this, especially in the earlier periods of 1904–29 and 1930–45. Efforts after that were more formal, but could hardly be called unsuccessful as the company helped the people of Sugar Creek take pride in their heritage as a refinery town. The solidarity of the people of Sugar Creek was manifested by the refinery, as evidenced throughout this case study.

One question that might be asked is: Would the outcome— that is, the demise of the refinery in Sugar Creek—have been different if the company had practiced public and community relations even more fully in the spirit advocated in this book? This is unanswerable in any definitive way. In fact, the question may be irrelevant. Our concern was not with business survival but with what could be learned from the Sugar Creek and Standard Oil experience. As far as the refinery is concerned, external factors—especially the economy of the oil industry—might have produced the same results. As for Sugar Creek, a greater sense of community among the residents might have reduced certain anxieties.

What the case study indicates is that much of what the Chicago School had to say is directly relevant to the practice of community relations, not as it is routinely practiced today nor as it is presented theoretically in the traditional literature, but as it could be practiced with an overall goal of restoration and maintenance of community. The Chicago School's theoretical framework is directly applicable to community relations and, more broadly based, to public relations.

The practice of public and community relations thus becomes quite straightforward. It is a role of communication as that concept was used by the Chicago School. It is a humane and altruistic function, but one based on a sound and pragmatic philosophy. It is a role, to a very great extent, of nonmanipulation. Too, it is a role that, if practiced as espoused here, should result in a more humane and mutually supportive society.

In a 1984 article exploring public relations and its social impact on the community, David J. Byrnes refers to a little-noticed side effect of public relations. That is to promote understanding of society and community through its communication function. With a concerted effort, he suggests, public relations could do much more than it presently does to alleviate ignorance, misunderstanding, and alienation.[72] We agree.

We would like to see the ideas of the Chicago School applied to other specialized areas of public relations. For example, can the restoration and maintenance of community as a primary goal of public relations practitioners and their organizations be applied to the media public? To the employee and member publics? To the publics in the focus of governmental relations? To activist publics? Another question: Can a sense of community be developed and maintained where it has never before existed?

We think that the theories presented here are applicable in many, if not all, of the other publics that public relations practitioners deal with. After all, a common, although sometimes unrecognized, reason for an employee publication is to create a sense of community, that is, a sense of primary reference group association, among the employees of an organization. Many of the other special publics can be absorbed into the building of the type of community that we advocate. Perhaps there are some publics that do not lend themselves to the theoretical applications set forth here. Frankly, we cannot think of any. Perhaps other scholars will be interested in applying the theoretical framework, or at least some of the concepts, to the many other publics with which the practitioner must be concerned.

Also worthy of closer examination is the relationship between the origin and evolution of public relations and the social changes contributing to loss of community. Did public relations step in to fill a communication void during this time? Our evidence suggests that this was the case. The question is worth further study.

At the beginning of this journey, we suggested that our recommendations for the practice of public and community relations might be radical or naive or both and, for some, overly theoretical. Our suggestions are radical only in the sense that they advocate a refocusing of efforts, that is, more conscientious and sustained attempts on the part of public relations practitioners to help their organizations and their communities restore and maintain desirable elements from an earlier social life.

Based on the case study reported, we would disagree with

allegations of naivete. We would much rather answer to the charge of idealism. The suggestions grow out of an idealism that we hope many public relations practitioners share. The suggestions we offer tend to be abstract, but the theory in which they are rooted is more intelligible and defensible than are most of the theories espoused in today's public relations literature.

Finally, we hope that future practitioners will continue to do what conscientious and progressive-minded practitioners should always be doing, that is, constantly reexamining their role and the larger social role of public relations.

Notes for Part III

1. Werner J. Severin with James W. Tankard, Jr., *Communication Theories: Origins, Methods, Uses*, 2nd ed. (New York: Longman, 1988), p. 24.

2. Clifford G. Christians and James W. Carey, "The Logic and Aims of Qualitative Research," in *Research Methods in Mass Communication*, Guido H. Stempel III and Bruce H. Westley, eds. (Englewood Cliffs, N.J.: Prentice-Hall, Inc., 1981), p. 358.

3. Ibid., p. 348.

4. Robert E. Park, *On Social Control and Collective Behavior: Selected Papers*, Ralph H. Turner, ed. (Chicago: University of Chicago Press, 1967), p. xxiii.

5. Ernest W. Burgess and Donald J. Bogue, "The Delinquency Research of Clifford R. Shaw and Henry D. McKay and Associates: Abstract Prepared by the Editors," in *Contributions to Urban Sociology*, Ernest W. Burgess and Donald J. Bogue, eds. (Chicago: University of Chicago Press, 1964), p. 601.

6. Jean-Jacques Rousseau, *The Social Contract*, Maurice Cranston, trans. (Middlesex, England: Penguin Books, 1968), p. 137.

7. Daniel J. Boorstin, *The Americans: The Democratic Experience* (New York: Vintage Books, 1974), pp. 48–49.

8. Ibid., pp. 49–50.

9. Amoco Oil Company, *Blazing New Trails, The Story of the Amoco Oil Co.* (undated publication).

10. Ibid.

11. Boorstin, *The Americans: The Democratic Experience*, p. 50.

12. Ibid., pp. 50–51.

13. Ibid., p. 419.

14. Amoco, *Blazing New Trails, The Story of the Amoco Oil Co.*

15. Ibid.

16. Paul H. Giddens, *Standard Oil Company (Indiana): Oil Pioneer of the Middle West* (New York: Appleton-Century-Crofts, Inc., 1955), p. 68. Giddens is one of the chief historians of the oil industry. Standard Oil financially supported the work on this book with the understanding that the author had complete independence.

17. Ibid., pp. 68–69.

18. Ibid., p. 69.

19. Ibid., p. 69.

20. Material about Sugar Creek comes largely from personal interviews with residents and visits by one of the authors to the community. When interview quotations, direct or indirect, are used, names of individuals are not given for purposes of protecting confidentiality.

21. Giddens, *Standard Oil Company (Indiana): Oil Pioneer of the Middle West*, pp. 68–69.

22. G. W. Thompson, "Pioneering at Sugar Creek," taken from Stanolind Record Book dated 1919.

23. See Bill Allison, ed., *Golden Memories of the City of Sugar Creek, Mo., Honoring Her 50th Anniversary Year 1920–1970* (Sugar Creek, Mo.: City of Sugar Creek, 1970), p. 3; and "Sugar Creek a City," *Independence* (Mo.) *Examiner*, 15 November 1920, p. 1.

24. As an example of these contrasting views, compare an editorial headlined "Standard Oil and Cement Good for Independence," *Independence* (Mo.) *Examiner*, 22 May 1905, p. 2, with a story datelined Chanute, Kansas, less than a month later, which the newspaper had picked up from another source. It spoke of a competing company's inability to sell more than one tank of oil a month, and the Independence newspaper's headline blamed the problem on "Standard Oil Oppression," *Independence* (Mo.) *Examiner*, 8 June 1905, p. 2.

25. Among newspaper articles telling about pollution problems and early attempts to resolve the problems are: "Finds S. O. to Blame," *Independence* (Mo.) *Examiner*, 2 February 1920, p. 1; "Standard Oil Will Help," *Independence* (Mo.) *Examiner*, 3 March 1920, p. 1; "Standard on the Job," *Jackson* (County, Mo.) *Examiner*, 19 November 1920, p. 5; "Pumping Its Own Water," *Independence* (Mo.) *Examiner*, 24 May 1921, p. 1; and "Standard Again Pumping," *Independence* (Mo.) *Examiner*, 3 June 1921, p. 1.

26. "Fire at Sugar Creek," *Independence* (Mo.) *Examiner*, 30 January 1908, p. 1.

27. "Independence Doesn't Want Standard Oil Punished," *Independence* (Mo.) *Examiner*, 28 January 1909, p. 1.

28. Beginning March 26, 1919, the *Independence* (Mo.) *Examiner* began publishing a series of institutional advertisements, which also ran in newspapers throughout the Midwest. The ads, which were used all through the next decade, covered a range of topics relating to Standard Oil (Indiana). The first ad asked, "Do you, or do you not, believe it [Standard] to be an institution which has performed its function of public servant in a manner satisfactory to the world at large and beneficial to every individual in it?" Standard Oil took partial credit for making Americans the best educated persons in the world, increasing property values, increasing production, assisting in each individual's pleasure, expanding business, and alleviating the suffering of humanity in general. The advertisement went on: "To this end the Standard Oil Company of Indiana, through the medium of this newspaper, will present a different phase of its business each week." The first advertisement was titled "What Do You Know about Standard Oil?" See *Independence* (Mo.) *Examiner*, 26 March 1919, p. 3.

29. See "Col. Stewart Talks," *Independence* (Mo.) *Examiner*, 2 February 1928, p. 1; and "Stewart Is Indicted," *Independence* (Mo.) *Examiner*, 2 March 1928, p. 1. The official was Col. Robert W. Stewart, chairman of Standard Oil (Indiana).

30. Interview with E. Conger Reynolds by Paul H. Giddens, 29 November 1969, pp. 7–8. Part of Conger Reynolds Collection, University of Iowa Main Library.

31. "Refinery Employees All Go on Full Time," *Independence* (Mo.) *Examiner*, 5 April 1932, p. 2.

32. "Standard Oil to Celebrate," *Independence* (Mo.) *Examiner*, 2 August 1935, p. 1.

33. "A Loan Is Repaid," *Independence* (Mo.) *Examiner*, 31 December 1937, p. 1.

34. "Retired from Standard," *Independence* (Mo.) *Examiner*, 2 June 1938, p. 1.

35. "Standard Oil Is Fifty Years Old," *Independence* (Mo.) *Examiner*, 27 June 1939, p. 3.

36. "Injuries in Blast at the Standard Oil," *Independence* (Mo.) *Examiner*, 18 July 1939, p. 1.

37. "Sugar Creek Ticket In," *Independence* (Mo.) *Examiner*, 2 April 1941, p. 3.

38. "Standard Oil Opposes Limits Extension," *Independence* (Mo.) *Examiner*, 30 March 1945, p. 1.

39. Amoco, *Blazing New Trails, The Story of the Amoco Oil Co.*

40. "Reynolds, Retiring from Standard Oil, Reviews PR Changes," *Advertising Age* 27 (23 January 1956): 8.

41. "Report to Our Neighbors," advertisement, *Independence* (Mo.) *Examiner*, 14 February 1956, sec. 2, p. 12.

42. "A Giant in Sugar Creek's Midst," *Kansas City Star*, 10 January 1957, p. 7.

43. "Standard Oil Steadying Hand in Community," *Independence* (Mo.) *Examiner*, 16 October 1957, p. 1.

44. "Business Citizenship," *Reactor* (July 1959): 4.

45. "A Refinery Is Tied by Strike of 750," *Kansas City Star*, 8 July 1959, p. 3A.

46. "Back to Work at Sugar Creek," *Standard Torch* (April 1960): 1.

47. "Strike Cuts Trade in Sugar Creek," *Kansas City Star*, 20 September 1959, p. 9A.

48. "Bitterness Divides a Strike Bound Town," *Kansas City Star*, 21 February 1960, p. 4A.

49. "Back to Work at Sugar Creek," p. 1.

50. "The Fifth Junior Achievement Program . . . ," *Reactor* (September 1960): 4.

51. "Refinery United Campaign Committee . . . ," *Reactor* (October 1960): 2.

52. "The Sugar Creek Refinery Was Host . . . ," *Reactor* (November 1960): 3.

53. "The Giant 16-Story 'Christmas Tree' at the Refinery . . . ," *Reactor* (December 1960): 1.

54. "It's Now American Oil Refinery," *Independence* (Mo.) *Examiner*, 13 January 1961, p. 7.

55. "Nearly 42,000 Readers . . . ," *Reactor* (February 1961): 3.

56. "Your Sugar Creek Refinery Has Set the Pace in the Oil Industry," advertisement, *Independence* (Mo.) *Examiner*, 28 February 1961, p. 3A.

57. See "A Quiet 75th Birthday by Standard of Indiana," *Kansas City Star*, 18 June 1964, p. 36; and "A Diamond Jubilee for Standard Oil," *Kansas City Star*, 25 June 1964, p. 40.

58. See "American Marks 60th Anniversary at Sugar Creek," *Torch and Oval* (November 1964): 2; and "Issue Permit for Duplex on Brent," *Inter-City News* (Independence, Mo.), 23 October 1964, p. 1.

59. An example of refinery publicity about the company's efforts to resolve such problems was the story headlined "Water Conservation Facility at Refinery an Industry Showpiece," *Reactor* (October 1966): 2.

60. "The Other Side of Pollution," *Observer* (Independence, Mo.), 29 April 1970, p. 1.

61. "American Oil Adds Anti-Pollution Unit," *Independence* (Mo.) *Examiner*, 9 January 1971, p. 4.

62. "EPA Seeks Charges in Delay by Amoco in Reporting Spill," *Kansas City Star*, 14 March 1978, p. 3A.

63. "Refinery to Reduce Odors," *Kansas City Star*, 27 June 1978, p. 4.

64. "Amoco: New Name Same High Quality," *Independence* (Mo.) *Examiner*, 20 February 1973, p. 2F.

65. Many stories dealt with the assessment disagreement, including "Proposed 60% Tax Increase Shocks Refinery—Company Appeals to State Board," *Reactor* (August 1971): 2; "Reversal in Assessment Sought by American Oil," *Independence* (Mo.) *Examiner*, 11 January 1972, p. 2; "Amoco Displeased in Tax Case Delay," *Independence* (Mo.) *Examiner*, 26 July 1973, p. 2; "Optimism on Tax Case," *Kansas City Star*, 13 November 1973, p. 4; and "Oil Firm Valuation Reached," *Kansas City Times*, 11 April 1974, p. 13D.

66. "Grant Helps Ethnic Groups Rediscover Heritage," *Kansas City Star*, 3 May 1979, p. 1E.

67. "Bibliography (sic): 'The Life of Mayor Rudy Roper'," *Independence* (Mo.) *Examiner*, 3 May 1981, p. 1.

68. "Sugar Creek's Refinery," *Kansas City Times*, 5 March 1982, p. A14.

69. Among sources explaining the company's rationale for closing the refinery were the documents "Remarks to Employees," by Refinery Manager George R. Helffrich, Amoco Oil Co., 3 March 1982; and "News Release" by Jerry W. Cooper, Amoco Oil Co., 1 June 1982.

70. "Sugar Creek's Refinery," *Kansas City Times*, 5 March 1982, p. A14.

71. "Amoco Plant Steeped in Family Histories," *Kansas City Star*, 7 March 1982, p. 29A.

72. David J. Byrnes, "The Public Relations Role for a Society in Conflict," *Public Relations Journal* 40 (July 1984): 12–14.

Bibliography

This bibliography contains citations as well as additional works related to the thesis of the book. It is designed for those who want to pursue specific subjects in greater depth. There are four main divisions: Public Relations, Community, Research Methodology, and Standard Oil Company (Indiana) and Sugar Creek.

PUBLIC RELATIONS

Books

Aronoff, Craig E., and Baskin, Otis W. *Public Relations: The Profession and the Practice*. St. Paul, Minn.: West Publishing Co., 1983.

Awad, Joseph F. *The Power of Public Relations*. New York: Praeger, 1985.

Bernays, Edward L. *Public Relations*. Norman: University of Oklahoma Press, 1977.

Brody, E. W. *The Business of Public Relations*. New York: Praeger, 1987.

Cole, Robert S. *The Practical Handbook of Public Relations*. Englewood Cliffs, N.J.: Prentice-Hall, Inc., 1981.

Crable, Richard E., and Vibbert, Steven L. *Public Relations As Communication Management*. Edina, Minn.: Bellwether Press, 1986.

Cutlip, Scott M., Center, Allen H., and Broom, Glen M. *Effective Public

Relations. 6th ed. Englewood Cliffs, N.J.: Prentice-Hall, Inc., 1985.

Dominick, Joseph R. *The Dynamics of Mass Communication.* 2nd ed. New York: Random House, 1987.

Dunn, S. Watson. *Public Relations: A Contemporary Approach.* Homewood, Ill.: Irwin, 1986.

Goldman, Jordan. *Public Relations in the Marketing Mix: Introducing Vulnerability Relations.* Chicago: Crain Books, 1984.

Golin, Alvin. "Community Relations." In *Experts in Action: Inside Public Relations,* pp. 111–123. Book by Bill Cantor and edited by Chester Burger. New York: Longman, 1984.

Grunig, James E., and Hunt, Todd. *Managing Public Relations.* New York: Holt, Rinehart, and Winston, 1984.

Heibert, Ray Eldon. *Courtier to the Crowd: The Story of Ivy Lee and the Development of Public Relations.* Ames: Iowa State University Press, 1966.

Kurtz, Harold P. *Public Relations and Fund Raising for Hospitals.* Springfield, Ill.: Charles C. Thomas, 1980.

Lovell, Ronald P. *Inside Public Relations.* Boston: Allyn and Bacon, Inc., 1982.

Lovell, Ronald P., and Geraci, Philip C. *The Modern Mass Media Machine.* Dubuque, Iowa: Kendall/Hunt Publishing Co., 1987.

Marston, John E. *Modern Public Relations.* New York: McGraw-Hill Book Co., 1979.

Moore, H. Frazier, and Kalupa, Frank B. *Public Relations: Principles, Cases, and Problems.* 9th ed. Homewood, Ill.: Richard D. Irwin, Inc., 1985.

Nager, Norman R., and Allen, T. Harrell. *Public Relations: Management by Objectives.* New York: Longman, 1984.

Newsom, Doug, and Scott, Alan. *This Is PR: The Realities of Public Relations.* 3rd ed. Belmont, Calif.: Wadsworth Publishing Co., 1985.

1987 Bibliography for Public Relations Professionals. New York: Public Relations Society of America, 1987.

Nolte, Lawrence W. *Fundamentals of Public Relations: Professional Guidelines, Concepts & Integrations.* New York: Pergamon Press, 1979.

Nolte, Lawrence W., and Wilcox, Dennis L. *Effective Publicity: How to Reach the Public.* New York: John Wiley & Sons, 1984.

Norris, James S. *Public Relations.* Englewood Cliffs, N.J.: Prentice-Hall, Inc., 1984.

O'Dwyer, Jack. *O'Dwyer's Directory of Public Relations Firms: 1985*
(New York: J. R. O'Dwyer Co., Inc., 1985).

Olasky, Marvin N. *Corporate Public Relations: A New Historical Perspective.* Hillsdale, N.J.: Lawrence Erlbaum Associates, Inc.,
1987.

Pavlik, John. *Public Relations: What Research Tells Us.* Newbury
Park, Calif.: Sage Publications, Inc., 1987.

Peak, Wilbur J. "Community Relations." In *Lesly's Public Relations
Handbook*, pp. 69–85. 3rd ed. Edited by Philip Lesly. Englewood
Cliffs, N.J.: Prentice-Hall, Inc., 1983.

Phillips, Charles S. *Secrets of Successful Public Relations.* Englewood
Cliffs, N.J.: Prentice-Hall, Inc., 1985.

Reilly, Robert T. *Public Relations in Action.* Englewood Cliffs, N.J.:
Prentice-Hall, Inc., 1981.

Robinson, Edward J. *Communication and Public Relations.* Columbus,
Ohio: Charles E. Merrill Publishing Co., 1966.

Ross, Robert D. *The Management of Public Relations: Analysis and
Planning External Relations.* Melbourne, Fla.: Robert E. Krieger, 1984.

Seitel, Fraser P. *The Practice of Public Relations.* 3rd ed. Columbus,
Ohio: Merrill Publishing Co., 1987.

Simon, Raymond. *Public Relations: Concepts & Practices.* 3rd ed. New
York: Macmillan Publishing Co., 1986.

Wilcox, Dennis L., Ault, Phillip H., and Agee, Warren K. *Public Relations: Strategies and Tactics.* New York: Harper & Row, 1986.

Yarrington, Roger. *Community Relations Handbook.* New York: Longman, 1983.

Journal Articles

"After 30 Years," *Public Relations Quarterly* 22 (Spring 1977): 8–11.

Files, James A. "RACE: A Public Relations Process Model for Orderly
Planning and Efficient Implementation." *Public Relations
Journal* 38 (July 1982): 22–25.

Goldman, Eric F. "Public Relations and the Progressive Surge: 1898–
1917." *Public Relations Review* 4 (Fall 1978): 52–62.

Harlow, Rex F. "Building a Public Relations Definition." *Public Relations Review* 2 (Winter 1976): 34–41.

———. "Public Relations Definitions through the Years." *Public Relations Review* 3 (Spring 1977): 49–63.

————. "A Public Relations Historian Recalls the First Days." *Public Relations Review* 7 (Summer 1981): 33–42.

Koch, Arnold. "On the Street Where You Live." *Going Public* (March 1981): 52–54.

Olasky, Marvin N. "The Development of Corporate Public Relations, 1850–1930." *Journalism Monographs* No. 102 (April 1987).

————. "Public Relations vs. Private Enterprise: An Enlightening History Which Raises Some Basic Questions." *Public Relations Quarterly* 30 (Winter 1985): 6–13.

Peterson, Paul V. "Enrollment up 7 Percent in '86, Outstripping University Growth." *Journalism Education* 42 (Spring 1987).

Post, James E., Murray, Edwin A. Jr., Dickie, Robert B., and Mahon, John F. "Managing Public Affairs: The Public Affairs Function." *California Management Review* 26 (Fall 1983): 135–150.

Unpublished Paper

Kruckeberg, Dean. "Public Relations: A Re-Examination of Definition, Role and Function Based on Community Relations of the Standard Oil (Indiana) Refinery at Sugar Creek, Mo." Ph.D. dissertation, University of Iowa, 1985.

COMMUNITY

Books

Boorstin, Daniel J. *The Americans: The Democratic Experience*. New York: Vintage Books, 1974.

Boydston, Jo Ann, ed. *John Dewey: The Middle Works, 1899–1924*. Vol. I: *1899–1901*. Carbondale and Edwardsville: Southern Illinois University Press, 1976.

Burgess, Ernest W. *On Communication, Family, and Delinquency*. Edited by Leonard S. Cottrell, Jr., Albert Hunter, and James F. Short, Jr. Chicago: University of Chicago Press, 1973.

Carey, James W. "Canadian Communication Theory: Extensions and Interpretations of Harold Innis." In *Studies in Canadian Communications*, pp. 27–59. Edited by Gertrude Joch Robinson and Donald F. Theall, Montreal: McGill University, 1975.

————. "Culture, Geography, and Communications: The Work of Harold Innis in an American Context." In *Culture, Communication, and Dependency: The Tradition of H. A. Innis*, pp. 73–91. Edited by W. H. Melody, L. Salter, and P. Heyer, Norwood, N.J.: Ablex Publishing Corp., 1981.

Cooley, Charles Horton. *Social Organization: A Study of the Larger Mind.* New York: Charles Scribner's Sons, 1911.

————. *Social Process.* Carbondale and Edwardsville: Southern Illinois University Press, 1966.

————. *Sociological Theory and Social Research.* New York: Henry Holt and Co., 1930.

Coser, Lewis A. *Masters of Sociological Thought: Ideas in Historical and Social Context.* 2nd ed. San Diego: Harcourt Brace Jovanovich, 1977.

DeFleur, Melvin L., and Ball-Rokeach, Sandra. *Theories of Mass Communication.* 4th ed. New York: Longman, 1982.

Dewey, John. *Art as Experience.* New York: Capricorn Books, 1958.

————. *Democracy and Education: An Introduction to the Philosophy of Education.* New York: The Macmillan Co., 1916.

————. *Experience and Nature.* New York: W. W. Norton & Co., Inc., 1929.

————. *Intelligence in the Modern World: John Dewey's Philosophy.* Edited by Joseph Ratner. New York: Random House, The Modern Library, 1939.

————. *The Public and Its Problems.* New York: Henry Holt and Co., 1927.

Edman, Irwin. *John Dewey: His Contribution to the American Tradition.* New York: Greenwood Press, 1968.

Emery, Edwin, and Emery, Michael. *The Press and America: An Interpretative History of Mass Media.* 5th ed. Englewood Cliffs, N.J.: Prentice-Hall, Inc., 1984.

Francois, William E. *Introduction to Mass Communications and Mass Media.* Columbus, Ohio: Grid, Inc., 1977.

Hughes, Helen McGill. *News and the Human Interest Story.* Chicago: University of Chicago Press, 1940; reprint ed., New Brunswick, N.J.: Transaction Books, 1981.

Klapp, Orrin E. "Style Rebellion and Identity Crisis." In *Human Nature and Collective Behavior: Papers in Honor of Herbert Blumer*, pp. 69–80. Edited by Tamotsu Shibutani. Englewood Cliffs, N.J.: Prentice-Hall, Inc., 1970.

Lawler, Edward E. III. *Motivation in Work Organizations.* Monterey, Calif.: Brooks/Cole Publishing Co., 1973.

McKenzie, R. D. *The Neighborhood.* Chicago: University of Chicago Press, 1923.

Matthews, Fred H. *Quest for an American Sociology: Robert E. Park and the Chicago School*. Montreal: McGill-Queen's University Press, 1977.

Mead, George Herbert. *Mind, Self & Society: From the Standpoint of a Social Behaviorist*. Chicago: University of Chicago Press, 1934.

————. *Selected Writings*. Edited by Andrew J. Reck. Indianapolis: Bobbs-Merrill Co., Inc., 1964.

Nisbet, Robert A. *Community and Power*. London: Oxford University Press, 1967.

Park, Robert Ezra. *Human Communities: The City and Human Ecology*. Edited by Everett Cherrington Hughes et al. Glencoe, Ill.: The Free Press, 1952.

————. *Race and Culture*. Glencoe, Ill.: The Free Press, 1950.

————. *On Social Control and Collective Behavior: Selected Papers*. Edited by Ralph H. Turner. Chicago: University of Chicago Press, 1967.

Park, Robert E., and Burgess, Ernest W. *Introduction to the Science of Sociology: Including the Original Index to Basic Sociological Concepts*. 3rd ed. rev. Chicago: University of Chicago Press, 1969.

Park, Robert E., Burgess, Ernest W., and McKenzie, Roderick D. *The City*. Chicago: University of Chicago Press, 1925.

Park, Robert E., and Miller, Herbert A. *Old World Traits Transplanted*. New York: Arno Press and The New York Times, 1969.

Quandt, Jean B. *From the Small Town to the Great Community: The Social Thought of Progressive Intellectuals*. New Brunswick, N.J.: Rutgers University Press, 1970.

Rousseau, Jean-Jacques. *The Social Contract*. Translated by Maurice Cranston. Middlesex, England: Penguin Books, 1968.

Swanson, Bert E. *The Concern for Community in Urban America*. New York: Odyssey Press, 1970.

Taub, Richard P., with Taub, Doris L., eds. *American Society: In Tocqueville's Time and Today*. Chicago: Rand McNally College Publishing Co., 1974.

Tocqueville, Alexis de. *Democracy in America*. Edited by Richard D. Heffner. New York: Mentor Books, 1956.

Wiebe, Robert H. *The Search for Order: 1877–1920*. New York: Hill and Wang, 1967.

Williams, Raymond. *Marxism and Literature*. Oxford University Press, 1977.

Wirth, Louis. *On Cities and Social Life*. Edited by Albert J. Reiss, Jr. Chicago: University of Chicago Press, 1964.

Journal Articles

Byrnes, David J. "The Public Relations Role for a Society in Conflict." *Public Relations Journal* 40 (July 1984): 12–14.

Carey, James W. "A Cultural Approach to Communication." *Communication* 2 (1975): 1–22.

Jones, Charlotte. "Homelessness in Modern Society: Mead, Berger and Mass Communication." *The Journal of Communication Inquiry* 6 (Summer 1980): 17–30.

Unpublished Paper

Belman, Sheldon Lary. "The Idea of Communication in the Social Thought of the Chicago School." Ph.D. dissertation, University of Illinois at Urbana-Champaign, 1975.

RESEARCH METHODOLOGY

Books

Burgess, Ernest W. "Social Planning and Race Relations." In *Race Relations*, pp. 13–25. Edited by Jitsuichi Masuoka and Preston Valien. Chapel Hill: University of North Carolina Press, 1961.

Burgess, Ernest W., and Bogue, Donald J., eds. *Contributions to Urban Sociology*. Chicago: University of Chicago Press, 1964.

Christians, Clifford G., and Carey, James W. "The Logic and Aims of Qualitative Research." In *Research Methods in Mass Communication*, pp. 342–362. Edited by Guido H. Stempel III and Bruce H. Westley. Englewood Cliffs, N.J.: Prentice-Hall, Inc., 1981.

Davis, Dennis K., and Bavan, Stanley J. *Mass Communication and Everyday Life: A Perspective on Theory and Effects*. Belmont, Calif.: Wadsworth Publishing Co., 1981.

Homans, George C. *The Nature of Social Science*. New York: Harcourt, Brace & World, Inc., 1967.

Rice, Stuart A. *Methods in Social Science: A Case Book*. Chicago: University of Chicago Press, 1931.

Ross, Edward Alsworth. *Principles of Sociology*. New York: The Century Company, 1930.

Severin, Werner J., with Tankard, James W., Jr. *Communication Theories: Origins, Methods, Uses*, 2nd ed. New York: Longman, 1988.

Stouffer, Samuel A. "Quantitative Methods in the Study of Race Relations." In *Race Relations*, pp. 208–216. Edited by Jitsuichi Masuoka and Preston Valien. Chapel Hill: University of North Carolina Press, 1961.

Journal Articles

Carey, James W. "The Problem of Journalism History." *Journalism History* 1 (Spring 1974): 3–5, 27.

Fuhrman, Ellsworth R. "Theoretical Observations on Applied Behavioral Science." *The Journal of Applied Behavioral Science* 18 (1982): 217–227.

Tirone, James F. "Education, Theory, and Research in Public Relations." *Public Relations Review* 5 (Spring 1979): 15–25.

STANDARD OIL COMPANY (INDIANA) AND SUGAR CREEK

Books

Allison, Bill, ed. *Golden Memories of the City of Sugar Creek, Mo., Honoring Her 50th Anniversary Year 1920–1970*. Sugar Creek, Mo.: City of Sugar Creek, 1970.

Flynn, John. *God's Gold: The Story of Rockefeller and His Times*. New York: Harcourt, Brace and Co., 1932.

Giddens, Paul H. *Standard Oil Company (Indiana): Oil Pioneer of the Middle West*. New York: Appleton-Century-Crofts, Inc., 1955.

Megles, Susi, Stolarik, Mark, and Tybor, Martina. *Slovak Americans and Their Communities of Cleveland*. Cleveland: Cleveland Ethnic Heritage Studies, Cleveland State University, 1979.

Periodicals, Including Standard Oil Publications

Amoco Oil Company. *Blazing New Trails, The Story of the Amoco Oil Co.*. Chicago: Amoco Oil Co., undated publication.

———. Sugar Creek, Mo., *Reactor* (June 1959–April 1977).

———. *This is Standard Oil Company (Indiana)*. Chicago: Amoco Oil Co., 1980.

"Reynolds, Retiring from Standard Oil, Reviews PR Changes." *Advertising Age* 27 (January 23, 1956): 8.

Special Profits Issue of *Torch and Oval*. "New Crude Still at Sugar Creek," 2, 9 (1963): 2.

Standard Oil Company (Indiana). *Annual Report.* Chicago: Standard Oil Company (Indiana), 1981, 1982.

Thompson, G. W. "Pioneering at Sugar Creek." From Stanolind Record Book dated 1919.

Torch and Oval (June 1949-November 1965). Named *Standard Torch* until January 1961.

Unpublished Papers

Mallinson, Roy. "History of Roy Mallinson." Unpublished manuscript, written 3 March 1977.

Otto, Frances V. "To Be of Croatian Descent Is a Priceless Heritage; A Study of the Yugoslav People." Unpublished manuscript, Sugar Creek, Mo., 14 May 1979.

Interview

Reynolds, E. Conger. San Diego, Calif. Interview by Paul H. Giddens, 29 November 1969. Part of Conger Reynolds Collection, University of Iowa, Main Library.

Newspapers

Daily News (Independence, Mo.), March 1952–September 1956.

Independence (Mo.) *Examiner*, May 1905–December 1982.

Inter-City News (Independence, Mo.), October 1951–August 1970.

Jackson (County, Mo.) *Examiner*, April 1904–December 1927.

Kansas City (Mo.) *Star*, June 1939–March 1982.

Kansas City (Mo.) *Times*, April 1952–March 1982.

Observer (Independence, Mo.), April 1970–May 1973.

Pictorial News (Independence, Mo.), 25 January 1962.

Sentinel (Independence, Mo.), January 1952–December 1958.

Sugar Creek (Mo.) *Herald*, January 1946–May 1954.

Index

ABOUT THE AUTHORS

DEAN KRUCKEBERG is coordinator of the public relations degree program in the Department of Communication and Theatre Arts at the University of Northern Iowa. He has been an accredited member of the Public Relations Society of America for more than a decade and is active in that organization as well as in the Public Relations Division of the Association for Education in Journalism and Mass Communication.

He has taught journalism/mass communication/public relations at the University of Iowa; the University of Minnesota, St. Paul; and Northwest Missouri State University. He has been a public relations practitioner at Lutheran General Hospital, Park Ridge, Illinois, and an information specialist for the Agricultural Extension Service at the University of Minnesota.

Kruckeberg has a bachelor of arts degree in English from Wartburg College, Waverly, Iowa; a master of arts degree in journalism from Northern Illinois University; and a Ph.D. in mass communication from the University of Iowa.

KENNETH STARCK is a professor in the University of Iowa School of Journalism and Mass Communication, of which he served as director for 11 years. During 1986–87 he was a Fulbright Professor in the Department of Journalism, Graduate School, Chinese Academy of Social Sciences. He has also taught at the University of South Carolina, Southern Illinois University, and the University of Tampere in Tampere, Finland.

He has worked as a journalist at the *Commercial Appeal*, in Memphis, Tennessee, and at the *Herald* and the *Review* in Decatur, Illinois, and in public relations at Wartburg College in Waverly, Iowa. He is coeditor of and contributor to *Perspectives in American Studies: A Reader by American Scholars in China*, being published by Shanghai International Studies University, and coauthor of *Backtalk: Press Councils in America* and *The Critical Factor: Criticism of the News Media in Journalism Education*. His articles have appeared in a variety of journals and periodicals, including *Journalism Quarterly, Gazette, The Journal of Experimental Education, The Journal of Communication Inquiry, The Journalism Educator, Communication: Journalism Education Today, The Journal of Education*, and *Journalism Studies Review*. He is past president of the Association for Education in Journalism and Mass Communication.